THE ATLAS OF EXPERIENCE

First published in Great Britain 2000

Copyright © Louise van Swaaij and Jean Klare

English text copyright © 2000 by David Winner
Maps translated by David Winner and Isabel Verdurme
Original Dutch text copyright © 1999 by Ilja Maso and Saskia Sombeek

Grateful acknowledgement is made to Curtis Brown Ltd, on behalf of Winston S Churchill, 1940.

'Sex and drugs and rock and roll': words and music by Ian Dury and Chris Jankel © 1977 Blackhill Music Ltd Watner/Chappell Music Ltd, London W6 8BS. Reproduced by permission of International Music Publications Ltd.

'Singin' in the Rain': words and music by Nacio Herb Brown and Arthur Freed © 1929 EMI Catalogue Partnership and EMI Robbins Catalog Inc., US. Worldwide print rights controlled by Warner Bros Inc, USA/IMP Ltd. Reproduced by permission of International Music Publications Ltd.

Words by Leonard Cohen taken from the song 'I Can't Forget' by kind permission
Stranger Music Inc/Sony/ATV Music Publishing.

The moral rights of the authors have been asserted

Bloomsbury Publishing Plc, 38 Soho Square, London W1V 5DF

A CIP catalogue record for this book is available from the British Library

ISBN 0 7475 5047 6

Production by Theo Pasveer and IPP, The Netherlands
Printed by Neue Stalling GmbH, Germany

THE ATLAS OF

EXPERIENCE

Louise van Swaaij and Jean Klare

English text version by David Winner

BLOOMSBURY

An atlas never just shows you where you are, where you want to go to and how to get there. It also fires the imagination. Maps which chart rivers, mountains, towns, countries, far-away regions, oceans and continents can arouse intense feelings. An atlas combines reality and fantasy.

Maps evoke travel, exotic places and the allure of the unknown. Without a map, there would be no way to know precisely where you are. There is no 'here' without 'there'. There is no world without a map.

The Atlas of Experience maps a new yet familiar world. At first sight, the maps look like ordinary representations of far-away places. On closer inspection, however, you will realise that you are surveying our shared world of thoughts and emotions. This atlas is based on traditional cartography, but it substitutes the names of cities, rivers and seas for concepts, feelings and everyday experiences. Topographic concepts acquire symbolic resonance.

Cradled by the Bay of Wisdom, the Sea of Plenty and Still Waters, lies a familiar and barely traversible land with a capital, Growth, and airports, Escape and Freedom. Everyone's experience is reflected in this world. You will find beautiful regions and desolate ones: climb the MOUNTAINS OF WORK, survive the DESERT OF DESPAIR, visit the ISLES OF FORGETFULNESS, be inspired by the STREAM OF IDEAS, pass through border towns such as DOUBT AND FEAR. This strange island reflects that inexhaustible adventure and journey called Life.

Our intentions are serious, but you can take the atlas lightly.

You can't really take a plane to the world of Experience, of course, because you already live there. It's the place where you go through many changes on the way to Somewhere Else.

Jean Klare and Louise van Swaaij conceived and laid out twenty-one countries in the Experience. The maps show in detail the regions and cities of this world. Each depicts a different theme and is accompanied by the philosophical reflections of David Winner.

The maps are drawn in Subjective Projection and reproduced in Unimaginable Scale.

Set out now on your own intriguing journey through this special atlas and experience an original, refreshing and perhaps enlightening outlook on life.

CONTENTS

LEGEND

- Hamlet

- Village

○ Small town

● Large town

♜ CITY

◆ CAPITAL

IMPORTANT BUILDING,
OBJECT OF INTEREST

Darwin Lane   STREET NAME

LOVE   DISTRICT

BAY OF WISDOM   SEA

POWER STATION	⎯•⎯•⎯ PIPELINE
NOISE	▬ ▪ ▬ TERRITORY
SOUND	▪▪▪▪▪▪▪ BORDER
STORM	▪ ▪ ▪ ▪ LIGHT RAIL
FORTRESS	▪ ▪ ▪ RAILROAD
AIRPORT	⎯⎯ PATH
LIGHTHOUSE	⎯⎯ ROAD
FACTORY	═══ HIGHWAY
WATCH-TOWER	RIVER
PEAK	RIVER WITH FLOOD BARRIER
VOLCANO	H HIGH PRESSURE
SHIP OR FERRY	L LOW PRESSURE
SUBMERGED WRECK	FRONT
SUBMARINE	LAKE
RUINS	BUILDINGS
BRIDGE	

BEACH

FARMLAND   MARSHES

HIGHLAND   ICECAPS

MOUNTAINS   SWAMPS

MOUNTAIN RANGE   RAIN

DECIDUOUS FOREST   SHALLOW WATER

PINE-FOREST

CEMETERY   DEEP WATER

'And what are the dimensions of a revolution ...?'
'The dimensions, Your High Excellency?'
'Well, the length, breadth, and thickness, if you like it better.'
Lewis Carroll, *Sylvie and Bruno*

Map-making is almost as old as human beings. 'The origin of the map is lost to history,' writes John Noble Wilford in his book *Mapmakers*. 'No one knows where or for what purpose someone got the first idea to draw a sketch to communicate a sense of place, some sense of *here* in relation to *there*. It must have been many millennia ago, probably before written language.'

Early Europeans drew maps on their cave walls, he tells us. Eskimos carved maps of their coast in ivory. In the Pacific, Marshall Islanders used sticks lashed together with fibres, coral and sea shells to represent prevailing winds, wave patterns and islands. On the maps of wheel-less pre-Columbian Aztec Mexico, roads were represented as lines of footprints.

In the last 100 years, the process of making maps has changed beyond recognition. Photographs from planes (and later spacecraft) changed the way we pictured the physical world and made ever-more detailed and complex maps possible. Now, computers can generate 3-D maps – and allow us to travel through them cybernetically. New places were mapped too: the moon, our neighbouring planets, distant galaxies. Simultaneously, map-makers have depicted cyberspace, deep oceans, the core of the earth, and mapped the tiny solar systems made of sub-atomic particles.

Medical science long ago charted the basic structures and systems of the body: the cardio-vascular system and our bones and muscles; the nervous and lymph systems. Soon the human genome will be visible. Scientists have even begun to map that most mysterious place of all, the inside of our brains. The so-called 'God Module' is the part of the brain which flares into activity whenever we think of matters spiritual.

Maps are usually considered as functional objects. They explain our surroundings to us and show us how to get to where we want to go. Yet they have always been highly evocative artefacts too, charged with poetry and fantasy. Marlow in Joseph Conrad's *Heart of Darkness*: 'When I was a little chap, I had a passion for maps. I would look for hours at South America, or Africa, or Australia, and lose myself in all the glories of exploration. At that time that there were many blank spaces on the earth, and when I saw one that looked particularly inviting on a map (but they all look like that) I would put my finger on it and say, "When I grow up I will go there".'

In the Middle Ages, lands beyond the borders of the map-makers'-knowledge were shown as full of dragons and exotic monsters. *Treasure Island* would have been a dull book without its map of hidden treasure. In one of his short stories, Borges conceived 'a map of the Empire that was of the same scale as the Empire'. There's a similar idea in Lewis

Carroll's *Sylvie and Bruno Concluded*: a map of the country made on a scale of a mile to a mile. The map, of course, could never be used. 'The farmers objected: they said it would cover the whole country and shut out the sunlight! So we now use the country itself, as its own map, and I assure you it does nearly as well.'

Even the most mundane-seeming maps can possess extraordinary poetic power and clues to a place's memories and soul. In *Rodinsky's Room*, Rachel Lichtenstein and Ian Sinclair tell the true story of David Rodinsky, a tragic and lonely Jewish man in the East End of London who vanished one day in the early 1960s. Nearly twenty years later, his one-room home above an old synagogue was rediscovered as he had left it, but crumbling into dust. Rodinsky had been dragged to a mental institution where he had soon died. One of the most potent objects he left behind was a copy of the London A-Z atlas which he had marked with ink. Sinclair later became obsessed with it. He described Rodinsky as a 'psychogeographer' and wrote a second book about his maps called *Dark Lanthorns*: '[Rodinsky] bent the maps to fit his notion of how London *should* be — if he was describing it for the first time. Maps were prompts rather than definitive statements. If a particular page took his fancy, Rodinsky would attack the margins with his red biro. Other districts ... were of no interest to him and they were ignored. He was a taxonomist, breaking down the overwhelming mass of information into categories that excited his attention: prisons, asylums, burial grounds of children's homes, hospitals. These markings become a projected autobiography, a Dickensian fable of abandonment, destitution and incarceration.'

One of the most famous of all American posters was Saul Steinberg's map of the world as seen by New Yorkers (Manhattan looming large and everything else in the world receding according to its cultural distance from the island). Even austere maps cry out for playful experimentation and reinterpretation. In *The Great Bear* the British artist Simon Patterson reworked the map of the London Underground and renamed lines and stations after philosophers, artists and soccer players. Upside-down world maps depicting Australia and New Zealand at the top of the world, and Europe and America at the bottom, adorn many office walls in the Southern hemisphere.

Meanwhile as old concepts crumble and new ideas are born in politics, the arts, religion and other areas of our lives, we look for new ways to describe ourselves to ourselves. It was perhaps only a matter of time before someone had the idea of playfully fusing classical cartography with the world of emotions, ideas and experience.

In 1999, the book called *Atlas van de Belevingswereld* (Atlas of the World of Experience) was a publishing sensation in Holland, becoming essential reading around the country and selling 100,000 copies in its first nine months.

English-speaking readers shouldn't think of this as a guide book. It's just a friendly companion for the latest stage of your most important journey: your journey through life.

'I hold this to be the highest task of a bond between two people: that each should stand guard over the solitude of the other. For, if it lies in the nature of indifference and of the crowd to recognise no solitude, then love and friendship are there for the purpose of continually providing the opportunity for solitude. And only those are the true sharings which rhythmically interrupt periods of deep isolation.'
Rainer Maria Rilke — *Letters to a Young Poet*

'I don't have anything personal. Nothing of value. No, nothing personal. Except my keys ...'
That's the obsessively secretive Harry Caul speaking in *The Conversation*, cinema's most unnerving study of loneliness, voyeurism and technology. Harry is 'the best bugger on the West Coast', a technically brilliant surveillance expert who unthinkingly dabbles in the stuff of other people's souls, using his high-tech long-range microphones and electronic equipment.

Harry plunders other people's secrets; yet he keeps his own under lock and armed guard. When his landlady breaks into his home to leave him a birthday present, he feels violated and switches his mail to a post office box with a combination lock. When his mistress, Amy, says: 'I want to know you,' he reacts as if she were Hannibal Lecter and he Clarice Starling. Amy's questions are innocuous: 'Where do you live?' 'What do you do?' 'What's your phone number?' But Harry panics and scurries for cover: 'Why are you asking me all these questions? You never used to ask a lot of questions.' Locks can be picked, security systems breached. But the portals of Harry's heart are impregnable.

Harry Caul is a clinical case, but we all have our secrets. We need them. Our secrets are, in a sense, our truest, deepest selves, or at least, *keys* to our deepest selves. As children, we keep a secret diary and a secret hideaway to store our most private treasures. We have secret sweethearts and secret passwords. These secrets make us feel there is a part of ourselves that belongs to us alone. As teenagers, our bedroom is our inner sanctum and *no one* gets in without an invitation.

We live in a culture that has developed an insatiable appetite for secrets — as long as they are someone else's. In the universal *Truman Show* of the digital age, private intimacies are violated so brazenly and routinely we hardly notice it any more.

The American president and the British royal family were almost destroyed by illegally recorded telephone conversations. Paparazzi hunt the stars, and no biography is complete without revelations about its subject's sex life. This is the price of fame. Yet ordinary people have never been more willing to display themselves. Jerry Springer rules the airwaves and 40,000 people in Britain volunteered to be filmed twenty-four hours a day in the TV show *Big Brother*, a title which mocks George Orwell's nightmare vision of a world without privacy.

Harry Caul has a conscience. When he tapes an innocent-seeming conversation between two
lovers, he worries about the moral consequences of his work and falters — only to be broken by an Even Bigger Brother. Meanwhile, one of the last American books published in
the twentieth century was *I Listen*, a collection of private phone calls in which people
unwittingly reveal their tormented relationships and sexual secrets for the amusement of
the reading public. The calls were recorded illegally by a secretive 'techno music artist'
known only as 'Spacewurm' who told a newspaper: 'You have no idea how addicting it is
until you do it. Imagine being able to listen in on your neighbors, your friends and best of
all, complete strangers in other cities. It's so easy, that's the best part. If you're smart
enough to operate an AM radio you're half the way there. The other half is actually the
harder part: being able to justify what you're doing, being able to handle the things you're
hearing. For me, it's easy.'

Paradoxically, though, the more of these 'secrets' we hear, the lonelier and less connected to
each other we seem to become. This is because there is a world of difference between
secrets stolen and given freely as an act of love.

I will give you all my keys.
You shall be my châtelaine.
You shall enter as you please.
As you please shall go again.

When I hear you jingling through
All the chambers of my soul.
How I sit and laugh at you
In your vain housekeeping rôle.

Jealous of the smallest cover.
Angry at the simpler door;
Well, you anxious, inquisitive lover.
Are you pleased with what's in store?

D.H. Lawrence

SEA OF POSSIBILITIES

DEEP THROAT

Trust

Refuge

Witness Protection Program

Top Secret

Code

Plot

X-Files

STEALTH

Love

Fantasies

Caution

Hidden Flaws

Leaks

Painful Truth

Espionage

Strategy

Need-to-Know Base

AREA 51

CAMOUFLAGE

to Dark Fantasy

HUSHHUSH

p 17

'In formulating any philosophy, the first question must always be: what can we know? That is, what can we be sure we know, or sure that we know we knew it, if it is indeed knowable. Or have we simply forgotten it and are too embarrassed to say anything?'
Woody Allen

'Well, whaddya know?' Sounds like a throwaway line from one of the heavies in *On The Waterfront*? Probably is. But, like they say in *Airplane*, that's not important right now. The point is that this small-looking question is actually very big. What *do* we know? How do we know it? How come that the more we know, the more we realise how little we understand? What else do we want to find out? Before you rush to buy a copy of Immanuel Kant's *Critique of Pure Reason*, here are a few pointers.

Common sense may be 'the collection of prejudices acquired by age eighteen' (Einstein). Yet we know what we know and, much of the time, that's good enough. According to common sense, the sun rises in the east and sets in the west, going on holiday is good for us, being ill is unhealthy, lightning does not strike twice in the same place and everything has a beginning, an end and a reason (except for God).

Most of our essential wisdom is picked up when are very young. In *All We Really Need To Know, We Learned In Kindergarten*, the American writer Robert Fulgham showed how deep the simplest advice from grown-ups can be: 'Share,' 'Say you're sorry when you hurt somebody,' 'Put things back where you found them,' 'When you go out into the world, watch out for traffic, hold hands, and stick together.'

Schools don't always advance the learning process. One day in 1994, the novelist Nick Hornby sat down and wrote on a single piece of paper everything he could remember having learned at his English grammar school between 1968 and 1975 in his eight least favourite subjects: mathematics, history, biology, chemistry, geography, physics, religious education, and economics and world affairs. This, after some 2,000 hours of tedious study, was what he remembered:

> Maths: Area of a circle is y r 2 . Circumference of a circle is 2 y r. y is 3.14 (approximately). R = radius. The radius is half the diameter. You have to look up sine, cos and tan in a log book.
>
> History: The Chartists had six points: universal suffrage, secret ballot and four others. Mr Huskisson was run over by a train.
>
> Biology: You dissect a frog by snipping up its stomach. Petri dish.
>
> Chemistry: Bunsen burner.
>
> Geography: The name of my geography teacher was 'Boggy' Lee.
>
> Physics: — .
>
> RE: — .

Economics and world affairs (A-level): The name of the American pilot shot down over the Soviet Union was Gary Powers. Cost push inflation. Demand pull inflation.

Albert Einstein (who knew a lot about knowing) said: 'Education is what remains after one has forgotten everything one learned in school.' So if we already know the good stuff (and we're not going to remember any of the facts we learn at school) what kind of knowledge should we be trying to discover?

In Bergman's *The Seventh Seal*, as Death and the Knight play their lethal game of chess on the stony beach, Death asks: 'What are you waiting for?' The Knight replies: 'Knowledge ... What will become of us, who want to believe but cannot? And what of those, who neither will nor can believe? I want knowledge. Not belief. Not surmise. But knowledge. I want God to put out His hand, show His face, speak to me.' Philosopher Bertrand Russell said three passions governed his life: 'The longing for love, the search for knowledge and unbearable pity for the suffering of mankind.'

But knowledge can be tricky stuff. Ever since Adam and Eve took the first tentative step towards a recipe for Mom's Apple Pie, humanity has been torn between a yearning for ever greater knowledge and an instinct for comforting ignorance, which is never far from cruelty. The Church persecuted Galileo for his heretical belief (the crazy man thought the earth moved around the sun, rather than the other way around), and the Inquisition burned people who were interested in the 'wrong' kind of knowledge. The Nazis started by burning thousands of books and ended by burning millions of people.

Is knowledge always a Good Thing? There are things we find out and then wish we didn't know. In the myth of Pandora's Box, human curiosity unleashes all the miseries and evils into the world.

Even Einstein, who wanted 'to know God's thoughts' and urged relentless enquiry ('the important thing is not to stop questioning. Curiosity has its own reason for existing') occasionally worried about the consequences. 'Two things are infinite: the universe and human stupidity; and I'm not sure about the universe,' he observed. And towards the end of his life, he bitterly regretted that his work towards uncovering the secrets of the universe had also paved the way for nuclear weapons: 'If only I had known, I should have become a watchmaker.'

SEA OF FERVOR

P 20

Discovered
Presupposing
Unknown
Unbelievable
Covered-up
Experiment
Into-View
COINCIDENCE
At-the-crossroa
Radical
Evidence
Non-Fictio
Revela
Fusion
Cold
DEEP
SHARP-WITTED
Association
Verifica
Sidetrack
Hypothesis
Illumination
To-the-bottom
Test
Beaten Track
Analysis
Method
Awareness
Speculate
High Standard
SCIENCE
Dawning
Self-confidence
PUZZLE
INTUITION
Connection
Mystery
Side Issues
Orde
Self-organisati
UNDERCURRENT
Hysteria
Disord
Contemplation
Mirage
Icarus Airport
Raving
Madness
Proclaim
Delusions
Symbols
Stream of Ide

SCALE
10 20 30 40 50

In the Middle Ages, we believed our lives were controlled by Providence. In recent centuries, as the idea of God began to falter, we have come to believe we are the masters (and mistresses) of our own destinies.

No longer pawns in some higher game, we decide how to live and how to behave. Our choices in life are limited only by our own imaginations: 'I want it all, I want it all, and I want it now,' as the Queen used to sing. (Well, Queen, anyway.)

Yet, somehow, we still go through our lives with a feeling of dissatisfaction. We seized the freedom to do what we wanted – and then found we didn't quite know what we wanted to do.

This is partly because life is not a simple struggle between pre-destiny and free will. There is another life-shaping force at work: the power of habit.

First we have habits. Later, habits have us. As the Talmud says: 'At first, habits are as light as a spider's web, but soon become as strong as cables.'

Habit rules our lives except for two key periods, when we behave badly. The times when we are swamped by our hormones and our neuroses are adolescence and the mid-life crisis. These are the times in our lives when we turn on our habits with the fervour and unreason of wild revolutionaries.

As an adolescent, Graham Greene suddenly became so fed up with his dull life that when he discovered his older brother's gun, he felt inspired to play a deadly game. He had read how bored White Russian officers put a bullet in their revolvers, spun the cylinder a couple of times, held the gun against their temples and squeezed the trigger. The chance of death was one in five. Greene liked the odds.

In his autobiography, *A Kind of Life*, he recalled: 'I pushed the barrel against my right ear and pulled the trigger. I heard a clicking sound and when I examined the cylinder, I discovered that the bullet could not have fired. It was in the next chamber. I remember feeling awkwardly happy, like when party lights are switched on in the dark and tiny street. My heart was pounding in my chest and life was offering me endless possibilities.' He repeated the experience: 'At quite long intervals I started to yearn for another dose of adrenalin ... Gradually this anaesthetic started to lose its effect and the whole experience left me with nothing but the brute stimulus of excitement ... I said goodbye for ever to the anaesthetic while spending the Christmas of 1923 at home in Berkhamsted. When I administered the fifth dose to myself, it occurred to me that I did not even feel excited any more; I pulled the trigger with such indifference it was like taking an aspirin.'

Even Russian roulette can become just a habit.

When we drift through life's habitual comings and goings long enough, the crisis of middle age becomes inevitable. We are too old to rebel against our parents, so we rebel against everything else we hold dear instead.

In puberty, we rebelled to become older. In middle age, we misbehave to be young again. Shakespeare understood: 'Age, I do abhor thee; Youth, I do adore thee.' Where we once found excitement and new identities through our music and clothes, now we try to spice up our lives with a new partner, job, car or even a new nose.

For the middle-aged neurotic, the equivalent of Greene's pubescent pistol is probably the bottle of poison which Faust kept close at hand during *his* mid-life crisis. Faust only had to hold the bottle with the firm intention of drinking it in order to feel better:

> *I look at you, and my grief is reduced.*
> *I reach for you, my urge is soothed.*
> *The tide of the spirit ebbs away little by little.*
> *I feel guided towards the open sea.*
> *The water shines by my side.*
> *A new day tempts me to a new beach.*

Goethe's Faust was a fictional character with a romantic solution to his problems. He made a pact with the Devil that would keep him young for twenty-four years. The condition was that he would not become attached to anything or anyone, or if he did, he would go to Hell. Instead of making a pact with the Devil, other men suffering from mid-life crisis find girlfriends who are twenty-four years younger. That keeps them young too. But Hell is never far away.

But whatever we do, habits will get us in the end, for every action contains the germ of a new habit.

The life of philosopher Immanuel Kant was governed by habits. For most of his adult life, the author of *The Critique of Pure Reason* allowed himself to be dragged along in a whirl of social distractions, friendships and love affairs. Well into his sixties, he changed things around completely. His final years were controlled by reason and regularity to such an extent that the citizens of Königsberg could set their watches by his daily constitutional.

We leave with the illusion that we enjoy free will. We don't. We have habits. The trick is to pick good ones.

> *Sow an act and you reap a habit*
> *Sow a habit and you reap a character*
> *Sow a character and you reap a destiny.*
> Proverb

SECRETS

Clearsight

Vision

Revision

Survey

Judgement

To Secrets

Penance

Disgrace

Experiences

Drifter

Bittersweetness

Sour Grapes

Spite

D I G N I T Y

Confession

Look Back

Look out

Look At

Submerged

Guilt

Violation

Forgiveness

Foul Play

Debauchery

DRIFTING

Consult

Awareness
Greater Aware

Lapse

Power

Evil

Fickle

Consider

Bluster

Gossip

Smoulder

Trick

Look Up

Nervous
Laughter

Hesitate

PROPAGANDA

Look Through

Flown

FATAL ATTRACTION

A Lie

Turmoil

Attention
(not paying)

Untouched

Evasion

Hypocrisy

Implacable

Superstition

Thin Veneer

Unshakeable

Disbelief

Judgement

Wish

Censor

Vocation

Illusion

Mistake

BELIEF

Habit

Hope

Assumption

Ideals

SCALE

10   20   30   40   50

To Excuse

Belly-Ache

Brat

Naughty

Push

Splash

Cry

Mischief

Y O U T H

Tree House

Hide and Seek

See-Saw

Playtime

Discovered

Sly

Notion

Reservoir

Patience

cence

Purity

Purification

Conscience

Good

Cancel

Target

Learn

tue

Look Across

Unlearn

Look Down

Delay

Slacker

Duty

Challenge

Intention

Waving

Soon

Later

Opportunity

D O   I T

Formed

Plans

Overflowing

Submerge

Bragging

Bombast

Reputation

Top of the Pile

Drowning

Devises

Immediately

Reckless

Perhaps

Distrust

Risk

Gamble

Up to you

Can Buy

Damage

Look Over

Luck

Daring

Assure

COURAGE

Pride

Neglect

D O U B T S

C H O I C E S

Avoidance

R E A C T I O N

Crossing The Line

Fame

Decision

Reflection

Discretion

Guess

isillusion

Charm

Trust

CERTAINTY

Dependent

Tiny

Talent

HEART

Big Hearted

Emotion

PASSION

TO ASSURANCE

TO SELFCONFIDENCE

TO DINNER IS READY

HOME

p25

'The skeletons in the cupboard are coming home to roost.'
Tom Stoppard, *The Real Inspector Hound*

'Never play cards with a man named Doc. Never eat at a place called Mom's.'
Nelson Algren, *A Walk on the Wild Side*

Aunt Em had just come out of the house to water the cabbages when she looked up and saw Dorothy running toward her.
'My darling child!' she cried, folding the little girl in her arms and covering her face with kisses. 'Where in the world did you come from?'
'From the Land of Oz,' said Dorothy gravely. 'And here is Toto, too. And oh, Aunt Em! I'm so glad to be at home again!'
L. Frank Baum, *The Wizard of Oz*

'When I was home after my first tour, I'd wake up and there'd be nothing,' says the soul-ravaged, hallucinating Captain Willard at the beginning of *Apocalypse Now*. 'I hardly said a word to my wife until I said yes to a divorce. When I was here I wanted to be there. When I was there, all I could think of was getting back into the jungle.' The film which famously begins with 'The End' (the Doors song) is also haunted by homes and their destruction. When Willard watches his fellow Americans partying after destroying a village full of Vietnamese homes, he observes: 'The more they tried to make it just like home, the more they made everybody miss it ... The boys on the boat ... weren't looking for anything more than a way home. Trouble is, I'd been back there, and I knew that it just didn't exist any more.' When Mr Clean, youngest of the boys, is mortally wounded, the scene is made unbearable by the sound of his mother — the voice of his lost innocence and the home he will never see again — playing on a tape as he dies.

Home is a deep human need and a preoccupation. In childhood we need its security and love. In times of stress we ache to return. Psychoanalytic pioneer Erik H. Erikson, inventor of the concept of 'identity crisis', argued that children need a feeling of trust as they grow up. Yet even after an idyllic childhood, we all develop feelings of discord and nostalgia. Freud thought the paradise for which we long must be the womb. During the First World War, British tommies in the trenches sang with longing 'It's a long way to Tipperary / It's a long way to go. / It's a long way to Tipperary / To the sweetest girl I know. / Goodbye Piccadilly / Farewell Leicester Square ...' In *Jaws*, just before the giant shark attacks their tiny boat, Quint, Hooper and Brody sing: 'Show me the way to go home.'

Aching for home may be universal. But each person's home is unique and irreplaceable. 'I'm going to my home town — sorry but I can't take you,' sang Rory Gallagher. Some homes are mobile. Molluscs like Brian the snail in *The Magic Roundabout* carry their homes on their backs. The roving tribe rather than a physical location is home for a nomad. The Austrian-born American Henry Anatole Grunwald said home was 'the wallpaper above the bed, the family dinner table, the church bells in the morning, the bruised shins of the playground, the small fears that come with dusk, the streets and squares and monuments and shops that constitute one's first universe.'

Home may be where the heart is, but we have to leave one day in order to live and to grow. *The Jataka; or, Stories of the Buddha's Former Births* tells of a tragic tortoise who refused to leave his comfortable, watery home by the lake, even though he knew the lake would dry up one day. When a hot spell comes, he still refuses to move: 'I was born here, I have grown up here, and here is my parents' home. I cannot leave!' Instead, he digs a hole and hides, but is accidentally killed when the future Buddha comes digging for clay. Before he expires, the tortoise speaks:

> *Go where thou canst find happiness, where'er the place may be;*
> *Forest or village, there the wise both home and birthplace see;*
> *Go where there's life; nor stay at home for death to master thee.*

The ideal best thing is to leave home, follow your dreams and return enriched by the experience.

The Arabian Nights tells of a wealthy Baghdad merchant once blessed with a beautiful house and a fountain in his garden, who has fallen on hard times. Then he has a dream in which a mysterious figure tells him to go to Cairo where he will find a new fortune. He goes, but suffers only disappointment and hardship. Finally, when he tells a man in Cairo the reason for his journey, he is mocked: 'You idiot,' says the man, laughing. 'You foolishly travelled because of a dream which was nothing more than a meaningless hallucination. A man came in a dream too and told me about some house in Baghdad where a great sum of money is supposedly buried beneath a fountain in the garden. But I didn't go off on a wild goose chase. I stayed at home. Why don't you just go home?' So the man from Baghdad did. He went home immediately, dug up the fountain in his garden and discovered the treasure lying exactly where the man had described.

As Dorothy says at the end of *The Wizard of Oz*: 'If I ever decide again to seek my heart's desire, I won't look any further than my own backyard, because if it isn't there, then I never really lost it to begin with.'

SECRETS

Recognition

Reunion   Longing

S E A   O F   P O S S I B I L I T I E

Peek

Pigsty   H

The Wall   Filthy

Dirty Linen

Fly off the Handle

T R U E   N A T U R E   Norm

Wrongside of Bed

Sleeping
Slippers

Snappy

Bathtime

E M O T I O N S

Bawl   Cuddle
                            Humming

Birth

Mittens

Tickle

Red-handed

Running Water

Brat

P O T T E R I N G

Y O U T H   Tree House

Lost

Hide-and-Seek

HABITS

Discovery   Rummage

See-Saw

B A C K Y A R D

Playtime

Reservoir

Patience

Golden Oldies

Round the Back

THE

SCALE
10 20 30 40 50

SAFETY

DREARY WOOD

Decency

Traditional

Location Track

Sunday Afternoon

Endless

Habit

Overflow

Vigilance

SAFE HAVEN

To Reunion

To Distaste

Humdrum

Inside Out

Wayside

Luxury

Pastime

REGULAR

Hot Chocolate

Slurping

Tea Time

Dinner is ready

Kitchen

Toast

Greens

Mouth-
watering

The Dishes

Soon

Kettle

Apple Pie

Visitors

Farewell

Welcome

Mail!

Welcome

Showing the Door

Next Stop

THE COUCH

Ailing

Sprawl

Tidy

Pointless

Sipping Wine

Lost Course

Snug

Chez nous

Neighbours

Automatic Pilot

Comfort

Out Laughing

Smother

Poor Prospects

Lap

Security

Sluggish

Weak

SAFE

COSY

On the Doorstep

Impulse

FIRST IMPRESSION

STINKING

SWAMPS OF BOREDOM

ᵖ29

'Boredom is like a pitiless zooming in on the epidermis of time. Every instant is dilated and magnified like the pores of the face.'
Jean Baudrillard

'I spent a year in that town, one Sunday.'
Warwick Deeping

'The cure for boredom is curiosity. There is no cure for curiosity.'
Ellen Parr

Here are some boring statistics. Or, more accurately, some statistics *about* boredom, which is more interesting. The figures come from a study conducted by Cyber Dialogue, a New York-based research firm, and were reported in the January 1999 edition of *American Demographics* magazine:

21 per cent of Americans are regularly 'bored out of their mind'.

Most Americans respond to such boredom by switching TV channels.

44.4 per cent eat when they are bored.

27.3 per cent go for a drive.

8.9 per cent drink alcohol.

35.6 per cent feign illness.

19.4 per cent cancel subscriptions to boring magazines.

14 per cent take a vacation.

10.8 per cent have a haircut.

67.9 per cent say no time of the week is especially dull.

12.6 per cent say that Sundays are likely to be dull.

9.8 per cent say weekday afternoons are boring.

6.7 per cent are bored by week-nights.

1.9 per cent are bored by mornings.

33.7 per cent end boring relationships.

7.6 per cent cheat on their boring partners.

62.9 per cent of Americans are rarely bored.

16.2 per cent are never bored.

3.8 per cent seek counselling for boredom.

Bertrand Russell, the British philosopher, logician, essayist, social critic and author of books such as *Human Knowledge: Its Scope and Limits*, *The Conquest of Happiness* and *The Philosophy of Logical Atomism*, observed: 'Boredom is a vital problem for moralists since half the sins of mankind are caused by the fear of it.' Really half, Bertie? Precisely 50 per cent, you mean? Are you sure about that figure?

Suburbia-on-Sea

Suburbia Harbour

B O R I N G

Suburbia-West

Yearning

Staring

Standing By

Suburbia River

Into Space

Tridge

Lake of

S A F E T Y

Decency

THE DUMP

Fingers

Tappling

Traditional

Sunday Afternoon

Nothing

Endless

Wandering

Habit

Overflow

Shopping Channel

Humdrum

To Distaste

Apathy

R E G U L A R

Inside Out

Luxury

Lazy

Wayside

Tea Time

Pastime

Kitchen

p 32

Toast

Greens

Kettle

Apple Pie

S W A M P S   O F   B O F

Frantic

Wron

HOME

Soggy

Next Stop

Not

Ailing

Normality

Leak

Counter 1

Counter

Pointless

Reluctant

Desk

Coun

Lost Cause

Automatic Pilot

Counter 4b

C O L L A P S E

Counter 4

Poor Prospects

Sluggish

Lost Causeway

Wrong Queue

Weak

Ticket Office

THE VOID

SCALE

10   20   30   40   50

TO
IMPULSE

MUDDLE THROUGH

Suburbia North
Potter Around
Suburbia
Suburbia Falls
Suburbia Parkway
Tease
Suburbia-on-Routine
Been There
Soap Opera
Yawn
South Suburbia
Droopy
Miss
Mope
Open Endings
Drizzle
Virtue
Persevere
Wait
Swallow
Solid as a Rock
Tower of Strength
Extremely Boring Area
Couch Potato
Run its Course
SENSIBLE
Patience
Stifle
Looking Forward
To Adventure
Reception
Whine
In Conclusion
Not Relevant
ROUTINE
Indeed
In A Minute...
Point Out
In reference to
Minutes...
Matters Arising
Point 2
Well
Whereby...
Page 86
MEETINGS
Returning to
Agenda
Moving on
And now...
Where was I...
Stop
If We...
And more...
Sum Up
By the way
um...   er...
Point 1
Concluding
So...
Therefore
Finally...
Refer
As it were...
i.e.
Let's See
The Following
...
Point of Order
Halfway
Where were we...
Lights, please

RECOVERY

'Illness is the night-side of life, a more onerous citizenship. Everyone who is born holds dual citizenship, in the kingdom of the well and the kingdom of the sick. Although we all prefer to use only the good passport, sooner or later each of us is obliged, at least for a spell, to identify ourselves as citizens of that other place.'
Susan Sontag, *Illness as Metaphor.*

Mary Lindsay (wife of the Mayor of New York): 'You look nice and cool, Yogi.'
Yogi Berra: 'Thanks. You don't look so hot yourself.'

The seventeenth-century British philosopher John Locke knew what was important in life: 'A sound mind in a sound body is a short but full description of a happy state in this World,' he declared. 'He that has these two, has little more to wish for; and he that wants either of them, will be little the better for anything else.' Or as Trudy Bernard (my grandmother) used to say much more succinctly: 'You should only be well.'

We all want to be healthy, as well as wealthy and wise. But it's easier said than done. After many centuries of medical research and countless generations of folk wisdom, we have begun to understand some of the basic ingredients of a healthy life. As long as you keep regular hours, eat a good and balanced diet, get plenty of exercise, think positive thoughts, avoid too much stress and have sex safely, you're in with a fair chance of being healthy. You should also try to get yourself some good genes and always stay clear of poisons, hostile micro-organisms, guns, wars, crime, fast cars, grizzly bears, earthquakes, exploding volcanoes and bad luck.

In *Sleeper*, Miles Monroe, owner of the Happy Carrot health food store in Greenwich Village, goes to hospital for a minor operation, wakes up 200 years later and finds it hard to believe that all his old friends have died: 'But they all ate organic rice!' In the twenty-second century Miles learns that things we think are bad for us (smoking, fatty foods, etc) are in fact ultra-healthy. The postmodernist cultural critic Richard Klein, debunker of health fads and author of the books *Cigarettes Are Sublime* and *Eat Fat*, has developed a similar thesis. As well as causing lung cancer, heart disease and many other horrible fatal illnesses, Klien insists: 'Smoking is praying ... The moment of taking a cigarette allows one to open a parenthesis in the time of ordinary experience, a space and time of heightened attention that give rise to a feeling of transcendence, evoked through the ritual of fire, smoke, cinder connecting hands lungs, breath, and mouth. It procures a little rush of infinity.' He has also argued: 'Life itself is a progressive disease from which we only recover posthumously; for if health is freedom from disease, then it is only available by dying. Living means choosing your poisons.' The tendency to ignore long term risks and live for the momentary pleasure of our vices can be irresistible. As Walter Bagehot said, 'The greatest pleasure in life is doing what people say you cannot do.' W.C. Fields knew the joys of keeping fit: 'Back in my rummy days, I used to shake for hours upon arising ... It was the only excercise I got.' The great film maker Luis Buñuel said: 'If the devil were to offer me a resurgence of what is commonly called vitality, I'd decline. "Just keep my liver and lungs in good working order," I'd reply, "so I can go on drinking and smoking."' And the Scottish folk singer Adam McNaughton is even more defiant in his song 'Cholesterol':

> *Well, I don't give a hoot for her yoghurt and fruit*
> *I'll have Black Forest Gâteau and die.*
> *Cholesterol, cholesterol, my chance of surviving is small.*
> *The way that I dine, I'm on course for angina, but I love my*
> *cholesterol.*

Even if you do want to do what's best, expert advice and the latest health research can be confusing. Around the turn of the millennium, the American media reported research studies showing that oestrogen therapy could lower the threat of heart disease and reduce the chances of developing Alzheimer's disease. A few months later new headlines warned that oestrogen therapy did not protect women from heart disease or slow the progress of Alzheimer's. And what about wine? Alcoholism and drunken driving may be bad. But, according to recent studies, wine-drinking may (or may not) reduce the risk of developing some types of cancer, kill some bacteria which cause food poisoning, lower susceptibility to osteoporosis and reduce the incidence of gallstones. Meanwhile, the jury's out on H_2O too. Water may be the stuff of life itself. But it has also been implicated in the vast majority of incidents of drowning.

Solid as a Rock

Tower of Strength

Crisis

Tu

Agitation

Case

Sign

Exhauste

H Y P O C H O N D R I A

On Edge

Phobia

Maelstrom

Hot Water Be

Feverish
Complaint

Tests

Refuge

Indicated

Ulcer

Visiting

Facts

Wallow

Trouble

Lament

Relief

Figures

Affliction

Sickly

Observation

Quench

Dro

Withstand

Vomit

Groan

On the Mend

Plaster

Supp

W
H
I
R
L
P
O
O
L

Sweating

Cod-liver Oil

Moan

C A R E

Nursing

Pale

Side Effect

Tic

Chicken Pox

Medicine

Prescri

Elixir

Twice Daily

Vitamin

R E M E D Y

Ray of Hope

Bedpan

Helpless

Symptom

Surgery

Beaker

Needles

Panic

ER

Casualty

Siren

Q
U
A
R
A
N
T
I
N
E

Contagious

Emergency

CHAOS

ADVENTURE

SCALE

FROZEN WASTES

F R O Z E N
W A S T E S

S T O R M Y　　C O A S T

Tremble

Bare-headed

Downpour

Windswept

SHIVER

Whirlwind

Chattering Teeth

Fever

Sniffle

Ravaged

Delirious

Reserves

Warning Signs

Defy

Meanwhile

mmy

Struggle

UNCONSCIOUS

Knocked

Out

Gnashing Teeth

Get Well Soon

Suppress

Sharpthetee

ent

Going Under

Excuse

Smelling Salts

Revive

Sportsflag

Ruddy

Fit

Glowing

SHELTER

Resistance

Speed Ahead

You're frozen when your heart's not open
Madonna

The Queen in 'The Snow Queen', Hans Christian Andersen's haunting fable of aridity and the
healing power of love, dwells in a vast, empty, cold place in the far north: 'The castle
walls were built of driven snow, the windows and doors of piercing winds. There were
more than a hundred rooms in the castle; the largest of them extending for miles and lit
up by the lights of the Aurora. They were large and empty, icy cold and glittering.' At the
heart of this bleak place is a frozen lake, 'cracked into a thousand pieces, each exactly
like the others and each a work of art.' The Queen calls this lake the Mirror of Reason ...

In the story, Kay, a once-happy small boy, becomes hateful, callous and coldly clever when
his eye and heart are pierced by two shards from a wicked hobgoblin's magic mirror.
Later, Kay gets kidnapped (and kissed a lot) by the Snow Queen. She carries him off to
her icy domain and holds him in erotic thrall. She teaches him 'reason', promises him the
earth and sets him an infernal puzzle: if he can find a way to fit together the fragments
of the frozen lake so that they spell out the word 'ETERNITY', the whole world (and a new
pair of ice skates) will be his. This is, of course, impossible.

P38

Luckily for Kay, his childhood sweetheart, Gerda, who is brave, loving and generous, arrives
to rescue him. Gerda finds Kay in a dreadful state, blue with cold and still dragging
around large, sharp pieces of ice in his bleak 'game of reason'. The story continues:
'[Kay] sat quite still, stiff and cold. Then little Gerda wept hot tears, which fell on to his
breast, and penetrated into his heart, and thawed the lump of ice and washed away the
little piece of glass which had stuck there.' Kay bursts into tears of his own which wash
the second piece of the evil mirror from his eye. He is cured! Finally, Kay and Gerda
embrace, a sight which is 'so pleasing' that even the pieces of ice dance in celebration
and, when they fall exhausted miraculously arrange themselves into the letters of the
word 'ETERNITY'. Kay is truly free.

Intriguingly, the name Kay crops up again in *The Godfather*, that mighty twentieth-century
epic of cold reason and frozen hearts. Here, Kay is a woman – the girlfriend (and later
wife) of Michael Corleone, the film's tragic central figure. Francis Ford Coppola's story
is darker than 'The Snow Queen', though, and his Kay proves powerless to save the
man she loves during his journey from light to dark. At the beginning of the story,
Michael is her engaging, warm and boyish lover. He ends the film as a loveless liar, and
embodiment of cold, cruel power.

No magic mirrors are involved. Michael inflicts the damage on himself. We realise he's in
trouble the moment he tells his brother: 'It's not personal, Sonny. It's strictly business.' His tragedy is that he thinks he must make himself cold and strong in order to
protect the people and the family he loves. But his increasingly icy heart and chilly

logic take him in the opposite direction. He is clever but not wise. The killing of Sollozzo, the assassination of the heads of the Five Families, and (later) the slaying of his own brother, Fredo, may all ultimately be good for business. But they have the effect of a car crash on Michael's soul. His mafia 'Family' goes from strength to strength. His emotional family is laid waste.

'Revenge is a dish best eaten cold,' as they say in Sicily. (They speak in similar terms of suet pudding in Macclesfield.) But Dante Alighieri, in his *Divine Comedy* about Heaven, Hell and Purgatory, warned that sins committed with a cold heart were worse — and are judged more harshly — than identical sins committed in the heat of passion.

Meanwhile, a cold persona — especially when coupled with a rigid devotion to harsh religious rules — is a recipe for unhappiness, as two other children, Fanny and Alexander Ekdahl, discover in Ingmar Bergman's movie *Fanny and Alexander*. When their father dies, the children's mother, a beautiful actress, remarries. It seems a fine match: her new husband is a respected local bishop. But life in his grey, castle-like home becomes hellish. The icy Bishop talks of obedience and duty and dispenses harsh 'discipline'. He is incapable of giving or receiving love. His domestic tyranny is in bitter contrast to the vibrant, chaotic, love-filled creativity and warmth of the large acting family they have left behind. The story is semi-autobiographical — Bergman's father was a pastor and Ingmar's childhood was desperately unhappy.

Yet, the bishop — like the Snow Queen and Michael Corleone — should be seen as a tragic figure rather than an evil one. 'Cold' people are usually sensitive souls who have suffered — or inadvertently inflicted suffering on themselves. As a result of hurt or loss, they take flight, withdrawing from the warmth of others to avoid being hurt again. Sigmund Freud and Melanie Klein identified this 'freezing' process as 'ego-splitting' and attributed to it lots of unhappiness-perpetuating personality disorders, such as narcissism, schizophrenia and the inability to form healthy long-term relationships.

As a psychic destination, the Frozen Wasteland has very little to recommend it. Fortunately, though, you can avoid ending up there by taking three relatively simple precautions:

1   Whenever you go to New York, do try, if at all possible, not to murder a leading member of any one of the Five Mafia Families.
2   Always stay away from mirrors made by hobgoblins (check label on back to make sure).
3   Never marry a bishop.

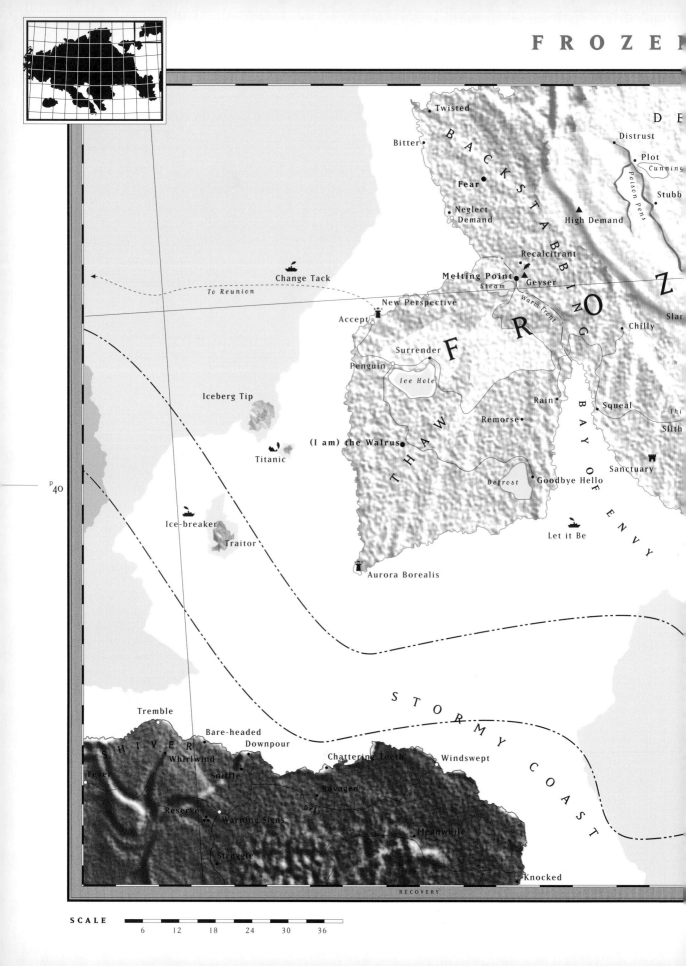

SCALE

6   12   18   24   30   36

Isolation

Insinuate

Exile

Rejection   Ignore   Indifference

Contempt

S T E S

Spine-Chilling

N   W   A   G   R   I   E   Absolute Zero

Mockery   V   I   Biting Sarcasm

Brittle   N   G

Break   Burning Hatred   Revile   Sharp

Bend   Taunt   Trembling

Shaking

Deathly Hush

ment

ing Teeth   Capricious   Cool   Stream of Poison

Fall   High Handed

Goose Bumps

Stab-in-the-Back

Icy Stare   Adrift

P
41

ash   Summer Ice

Winter Ice

As any compiler of lists of uplifting quotations will tell you, 'Genius is one per cent inspiration and ninety-nine per cent perspiration.' On the other hand, you can sweat till your washing machine breaks down and still be mediocre. You've got to have a Gift.

Think of all the hard-working musicians who perspire diligently for a lifetime without ever coming up with something like the 'Hallelujah Chorus'. Then consider the case of the man who wrote the 'Hallelujah Chorus'. George Frederick Handel's father was a barber-surgeon who hated music. He wanted his son to become a lawyer, and tried to suppress his talent, obliging George to practise secretly on a spinet harpsichord hidden in the attic, each string wrapped with thin strips of cloth. As a young man, Handel moved to England and wrote numerous operas and oratorios. He was successful and prominent, but he was also mocked because of his fatness and heavily-accented English, and he was often in financial trouble. By 1741, he was at one of his lowest points and was on the verge of returning to Germany. Then a friend, Charles Jennens, asked him to compose an oratorio based on a compilation of scriptures he had made. Handel agreed and began work on 22 August.

Handel composed the *Messiah* in twenty-four days without once leaving his house. During this time, his servant brought him food, and when he returned, found the meal was often uneaten. While writing the 'Hallelujah Chorus', Handel was found with tears in his eyes. He told his servant: 'I did think I did see all Heaven before me, and the great God Himself!' Around the same time, Handel became devoutly religious, and started going twice a day to church. Many years later, at a performance of the *Messiah* in honour of his seventy-fourth birthday, Handel was feted and treated to thunderous applause. He responded: 'Not from me, but from Heaven comes all.'

The *Messiah* may be one of the most sublime of all human works, but even at a less exalted level, the process of artistic creation remains profoundly mysterious.

At the age of forty, the sixteenth-century French politician and author Michel de Montaigne withdrew to his country estate, determined to worry about nothing except 'how to spend the rest of my life in peace and seclusion'. He set his mind the task of becoming 'totally idle' so that it could 'find its own peace' He was hoping this wouldn't be difficult, but he was wrong. 'The mind [which he called his "runaway horse"] gives itself many more problems than it could ever bear for another. It causes me to experience so many illusions and strange monsters, one after the other, without order and without sense. So I started writing them down to consider them in all their oddity and absurdity, hoping eventually to make it feel ashamed of itself.'

Unfortunately we don't have space here to explore the metaphysical conundrum of whether Montaigne and Montaigne's mind (or horse) really were separate entities (though Steve

Martin's *The Man With Two Brains* explored similar terrain). Suffice to say that over the next twenty years, Montaigne entirely failed to tame his horse/mind/brain combo. Instead, he wisely allowed it/them to gallop away with itself/themselves, and, in the process, all of them together invented the Essay. Montaigne wrote more than a hundred celebrated and influential Essays with such diverse titles as 'Of Glory', 'Of Cannibals', 'Of the Resemblance of Children to Their Fathers' and 'That to Study Philosophy is to Learn to Die'. Montaigne also made a key discovery. He found that, when we focus on matters of the spirit rather than on a particular subject, we enter 'the indefinable world of imagination'. There we find more treasures than we could ever have suspected.

Samuel Taylor Coleridge provides the most famous case of doomed inspiration. In the summer of 1797, Coleridge, who had taken opium because he was suffering from dysentery, read this unpoetic account of the Mongol emperor: 'Kubla Kahn decreed the construction of a palace with an imposing garden. And so far ten miles of the fertile soil were surrounded by a wall.' Then Coleridge fell into a fitful, drugged sleep. For three hours as he drifted in and out of waking, two to three hundred lines of a new poem came to him effortlessly in pictures and phrases. When he got up, he could remember the entire poem. He gathered pen, ink, paper and started to write:

> *In Xanadu did Kubla Khan*
> *A stately pleasure-dome decree:*

Then he was interrupted by a visitor from Porlock who insisted on discussing a business matter. Coleridge had to talk for more than an hour, and when he returned to his writing, discovered that, apart from ten lines, the poem had disappeared from his mind 'like the images on the surface of a stream in which is cast a stone'. Fortunately, this new metaphor triggered a succession of images that enabled Coleridge to reconstruct parts of the vanished dream. This time, there was no visitor and Coleridge finished a new version of the poem.

The story has become a metaphor for thwarted brilliance. In Raymond F. Jones's science-fiction story 'Person from Porlock', aliens watch for signs of human creativity and, when they spot some, immediately send a person from Porlock to subvert them. In *Dirk Gently's Holistic Detective Agency* by Douglas Adams, a lover of the poem goes back in time and stands guard at Coleridge's door as he sleeps, determined to stop his visitor. He waits and waits and no one appears. Finally, worried, he knocks at the door to find out if anyone has somehow got past him ... and realises that he himself has become the Person from Porlock. The point is that genius or even genuine creativity (in whatever field) remains fragile and elusive. When it happens successfully, it ought to be celebrated. In song, perhaps, with an orchestra and a big choir ...

U N D E R C U R R E N T

Side

Hysteria
• Contemplation

Illusion
Madness
• Icarus Airport
Raving

Delusions

Symbol

I R R A T I O N A L

✈ Flights of Fancy

Similarities

Extreme

Utmost

Parado

Clarity

Opposite

One Hand

C O L O U R S

Intensity

Taste

The Other

Birds-eye View

S E A   O F   F E R V O U R

Jealousy

Reckless Heights

Fiery
Blazing
Sparksfly
Ardour

Turbulent
Surrender
Overwhelming

Ecstasy
Stormy

VULNERABLE

Tender

VOLCANOES OF PASSION

SCALE

0,1   0,2   0,3

Order

COMPOSITION

Invention

Fiddle

roclaim

Connection

Design

CREATIVITY

ich Ideas

Repetition

Opinion

Perceive

Impulse

MOODS

subconscious

Sparks

ment

SOUND

Flowing On

Observation

Scent

Melody

Transparent

FRAGMENTS

Lovebirds

Change

Move

Recognition

Notes

Symphony

oposite

Solution

Concentration

CREATION

Transcontinental pipeline of transformation

ARTS

Startle

Reflection

SOURCES OF INSPIRATION

Past

FINE

relevant

Mixing

Anxiety

Present

Promise

Sink In

Floating

Eloquence

Notion

PASSION

Idea

Humour

Awakenings

Concept

FEELINGS

BLOOMING

Rendez-Vous

Development

Frustration

FERTILE

stream of words

Good Idea

Stream of Inspiration

Ugly

Beautiful

Smile

Laughter

EXPORT

Hate

Silence

Kiss

IMPORT

BEYOND

WORDS

Speechless

Expedition

The Light

THE ISLES OF
FORGETFULNESS MAP 9

And I can't forget
I can't forget
I can't forget
But I don't remember what
Leonard Cohen.

According to a legend from the Talmud, children in the womb are wise beyond words. They are taught the Torah and then all the secrets of the universe are revealed to them. But at the moment of birth, an angel strikes them on the mouth and makes them forget everything. There's a similar idea in Plato's *Republic*: souls arrive in the world as falling stars and then, on the journey to life, must travel through a desert. By the time they reach Lethe, the River of Oblivion, they are thirsty, so they drink deeply from its memory-erasing waters. Some souls drink so much they immediately forget everything of their previous existence. Others, who drink more moderate quantities, retain a vague sense of their past lives. (These souls, said Plato, were the ones able to pass on something of their wisdom later in life. They become the world's philosophers, lovers and artists.) Or as Wordsworth put it:

Our birth is but a sleep and a forgetting:
The Soul that rises with us, our life's Star,
Hath had elsewhere its setting,
And cometh from afar:
Not in entire forgetfulness

To live is to forget. And it's better that way. If we remembered everything, our minds would be a nightmarish clutter. There have been cases recorded of people who forgot so little that their everyday lives were totally confused. There was no space for new thoughts or intelligent processing of information. Friedrich Nietzsche (how could we forget him?) believed that without forgetting there could be no happiness, no hope, no here and now. 'Whoever thinks much and to good purpose easily forgets his own experiences, but not the thoughts which these experiences have called forth.'

If people remembered everything, secretaries and diary manufacturers would be out of jobs. Moreover, the individual's tendency to forget has been one of the motors of human culture and creativity. Once upon a time, stories were passed down orally from generation to generation. Eventually there were too many stories to remember them all, so writing was invented to record them. Books came later. Then libraries, archives, data banks, and, eventually, the Internet.

If human beings were computers (which we aren't) we might compare our memories to hard-drives which slowly but surely fill up with old files and file fragments as we get older. And the older we become, the more difficult it gets for us to process new knowledge and experience. Older people remember events of thirty years ago more clearly than those of last week. The American writer and psychologist Lawrence LeShan observes that, for the first fifty years of our lives, we remember the details of the tasks we have to perform. But after the age of about sixty we see the world differently. We focus more on relationships and meanings. Our memory becomes more selective. Instead of remembering the names of the people we have just met, we focus on the emotional tone of the meeting. Instead of facts, we remember meaning. Instead of width, we remember depth. We lose the sharp edges of our memory; but that just makes us wiser and more able to put things into perspective.

Living is forgetting and forgetting is selecting. We come into the world as a blank page and leave it fully written. For most of us, absent-mindedness and oblivion are probably all we have to look forward to.

Don't remember where you put your keys? Don't worry. Think of it as your contribution to the advance of human civilisation.

I S L E S   O F   F o

ISLES OF Fo

Which Islands?

to Memory and Reminiscence

Whatever

Joke

Punchline   Lost

Nevermind   Fla

Time   Damn Ke

Departure   S

Lost Energy   Ehm...   Mn
                                          bri
Erm...

Hmm...   Fort Alzheimer   BLAC

              Er...   Fac

                                    Tip of the To

E T F U L N E S S

versary

Pincode

Mother's Day

HEMATICS
Yourname
Firstname
MES Surname
atshisname

TRAITS OF ...

tment

'To be able to say how much one loves, is to love but a little,' said Petrarch, spot on on the question of the incompatibility of scorching passion and taking a rational approach.

That's the whole point of passion: to be the total opposite of cool reason.

Passion drags us to the Realm of the Senses, a land to which Logic can't even get a tourist visa.

'You shake my nerves and rattle my brain / Too much love drives a man insane,' noted Jerry Lee Lewis, from the male perspective, in his seminal work, 'Great Balls of Fire'. A similar sense of delicious, exultant, scrambled senses emerges from the poems of Sappho: 'As soon as I see you, even for a moment, I can no longer utter a single word. My voice falters. I feel a sudden burning under my skin as if touched by raging fire. My eyes become veiled; my ears sing. I sweat. My entire body shakes. The world has turned a different colour and I am about to bid life adieu.'

Historically speaking, because of its power to disrupt lives and the social order, passion is never in fashion with moralists. They usually think of it as a menace to society.

The Roman philosopher Boethius, who reckoned the route to human happiness lay in the pursuit of wisdom and love of God, saw passion as poison: 'When [Lady Philosophy] saw the muses of Poetry surround my bed, dictating words to accompany my tears, she became angry. "Who," she demanded, her penetrating eyes blazing, "allowed these hysterical whores to approach the sickbed of this man? They have no medicine to ease his pain, only sweet poison to make it worse. These are the women who murder the rich and fertile harvest of Reason with thorns of Passion."'

Down the ages, philosophers, priests and psychologists have begged us — commanded us! — not to let ourselves be overwhelmed by our emotions.

Different religions, civilisations and cultures have tried various forms of rigid control.

In ancient Sparta, *all* expressions of passion were forbidden. Even married people were only permitted to make love in secret and it was as big a scandal to be found in bed with your own spouse as with someone else's. It didn't work of course. What could be sexier than arranging all those secret trysts and rendezvous? As Montaigne said: 'The risk of being caught, the embarrassment of the day after ... that is what makes it so fascinating!'

When all's said and done, we don't really need Passion Police. Some form of well-equipped emotional fire brigade would be much more useful.

CONDUCT

TO BELIEF

HEART
Dependence
Sweet Nothings
Ideals
Big Hearted
Emotion

CREATIVITY

HAPPINESS

Obsession

Boundless

Voyeur

Jealousy
Reckless Heights
Fiery
Sparksfly
Ardour
Blazing
Surrender
Ecstasy

Unconditional

Out of Control
Craving
Lust

Virtuoso
Nocturne
Serenade
LOVE
Scherzo
PLAY
Wavering
Turbulent
Stormy
Overwhelming

Symphony
Affair
Desire
VULNERABLE
Tender

Promise
Intense

Mistress
Glances
Sighs
Frolic

BLOOMING
Awakenings
Rendez-vous

Jubilant
Caresses
Fanfare
Enthusiasm

Appreciation
Propose
Energy

Ugly
Beautiful
GIVE

Hate
Smile
Laughter
EXPORT
Tête-à-tête
GROWTH

Farewell
MOUNTAINS OF WORK

Silence
Kiss
Wait
Stock
Margin

IMPORT

Pity
RECEIVE

The Light
Expectation
Stimulating
Frenzy
Uplift
Chance
Another chance

SAFE HAVEN

Impatience

PLEASURE

SCALE
10 20 30 40 50

MOUNTAINS
OF WORK

MAP 11

An old lady can take most of a day to write and send a single postcard to her niece in Littlehampton. It takes her an hour to find the right card, for a start. 'Where did I put my glasses?' That's another hour. Actually writing the card takes up to ninety minutes. There's half an hour to check the address, and the process of making a decision about whether or not to take an umbrella to the postbox can take another twenty minutes. So a task which would take a busy person no more than about three minutes leads to a day of frustration and effort. Thus the British historian and wit, C. Northcote Parkinson, illustrated his theory that 'work expands to fill the time available for its completion'.

Most of us know all about this 'Parkinson's Law'. We yearn for shorter working hours, more days off and longer holidays. We even look forward to our retirement because we know we can – at last – do all the important things we don't have time for now.

Yet when the golden day finally arrives, we are appalled to discover we still don't have time to learn Italian, visit art galleries or give the garden shed a good clean. This is because we spend all morning taking the dog to the vet and there were e-mails to answer – and that took all afternoon. What we used to get done in no time when we were busy people ('between acts', as the French say) now turns out to be a mountain of work. So we still don't have time for the really important stuff.

Meanwhile, over the last decade or so, as people with jobs have discovered, employers (who were a little slow to catch on at first) have applied the principles of Parkinson's Law. Never before have the few people who still have work had so much work to do. Fewer and fewer people do more and more work and where does that leave the rest of the population? Up to their ears in it, that's where – and the garden shed's *still* a mess.

Still, we mustn't grumble, must we? Having work is a privilege and isn't labour essentially noble? Well, not according to Xenophon, the ancient Greek historian, who viewed hard work with contempt: 'Handicrafts ruin the bodies of craftsmen and foremen, forcing them to sit still and live indoors and in some cases to spend the day in front of the fire. And the weakening of the body is accompanied by a serious weakening of the mind. Furthermore, these so-called crafts leaving no time to devote to friend and country, so that those who practise such have a reputation for being wanting in friendship and poor defenders of their homeland.'

The modern-day version of this view might be the line: 'Work is the curse of the drinking classes'. But Xenophon was way ahead of his time in spotting a connection between work and personality. More than 2,200 years went by before Hegel and Marx looked

P52

again at the concept. Hegel said (approximately) 'What you do influences who you are and as the other way around is also true.' Marx, in 1844, took the idea that stage further: 'If you are alienated from what you do you are alienated from yourself.' Marx felt that anyone who works for another would be alienated because he would belong to that other person.

This doesn't help us much today. Whenever we feel alienated from our jobs or our colleagues, we don't take the drastic decision to become self-employed. And we don't incite our fellow alienated workers to socialist revolution. No, we go off on a jolly team-building survival weekend in the New Forest. This supposedly enables us to discover ourselves completely and also improves our chances of survival within the company. We just get on with it.

Various factors shape our feelings towards our work at different times of our lives – the pressure and variety of the work itself; the state of our marriage, and so on. When work is a strain, we hate people who seem to work less than we do but earn more than us. We even resent the people who don't need to work or can't work. And we are especially jealous of people who enjoy their work so much it seems to be their hobby.

Contrariwise, when we are happy in our work, earning more seems a little less important and we view the unemployed people with pity and compassion. All of a sudden, our work has become our hobby.

We work too hard and others don't pull their weight. They earn too much and we aren't paid enough. When they fail, some get a golden handshake. Others are made redundant. Some people leap from one exciting job to another while others are stuck in hopeless monotony. Some people spend their lives sending out CVs; others get head-hunted. We survive all this and make it to our retirements. And then we have more mountains of work to look forward to – Parkinson's sort.

Perhaps there is nobility in labour after all.

NIGHTLY ACTIVITIES IN THE CITY OF STRESS

Self-confide

STRESS

Mobile Phone

H

H

TENSION

OVERWORK

PLAINS
SOLITU

Expectations

Lonely at the Top

Energy

Enthusiasm

Pros   Cons

Not my Fault

Mem
Gos

GROWTH

Escape

Call
Voicem

Jet Lag

Annual Results
•245
•139

Administra

Ambition

Driven

Fault

Fun

Responsibility

Delegate

Pro

Stock

Margin

Subterfuge

Initiative

Tasks

Choice

D
Pressu

Blood, Sweat and Tears

Compass Road

Chance

Hint

ACTION

Su

Mission Statement

Perceptivity

Power Freedom

Another Chance

Risk

Negotiation

Attention

Mouthshut
Arguments

Sign

Persuasion

Coincidence

Presentation

Big Mouth Fabrica

Affluence

Surprise

Disguise

Lie

All the Best

Fast Food

P R A C T I C

Leisurelunch

PLEASURE

SCALE

10   20   30

THE VOID

CHANGE

Somewhere

Consequences

THE VOID

Satisfaction

EMPOWERMENT

Turning Point

Come On!

Grin and Bear it

Wash

Washed Out

Sip

Foolishness

Exhausted

Finally

Completely Forgot

Broke

Again

Aspiration

Persistence

will

Grim

Impossibilities

ng Smoothly

Limit

AINS OF WORK

Ends Meet

Halfway There

Reluctance

Pie in the Sky

ESS

Drudgery

Delay

Mobile Phone
Overwork

Meetings

Niche [Marketing]

Feeble Excuse

Post

Castles in the Air

lm Down

PAYSLIP

Traffic Jam

Pillar

Failure

Receipt

THE GREEN GRASS

HARVEST

Bigger

Resign

WEALTH

Lake Plenty

Better

Facade

Jealousy

A Dirty Look

Past Glory

Decadence

Prosperity

ANTICIPATION

BACKWATER

Prospectus

Old Times

MORTALITY

GIVE

New Burning
Bridge

Laughter

Burning
Bridge

Spurt

Trade

RECEIVE

EXPORT

FORCE

Offer

Admit

Waiting

STORE

IMPORT

Godot

POTENTIAL

Expectation

Stimulating

S A F E   H A V E N

Rivals

Impatience

SCALE

10   20   30   40   50

PROLIFERATE

DEVELOP

Next Month

Spur Cn

Jet Lag

Jet Lag Terminal

EXPLOSIVE

GROWTH

SPIRE

EXPLOIT

Venture Structure

AMBITION

EXPAND

Day after Tomorrow

Tomorrow

SUPPLY

STOCK

MARGINS

STIMULATE

Firm

Next Week

nzy

ENCOURAGE

Seen

Uplift

Manana

Chance

Another Chance

Doctor: What kind of 'void'?
Boris: An *empty* void.
Doctor: An *empty* void?
Boris: I felt a *full* void a month ago, but it was just something I ate.
Woody Allen, *Love and Death*

Oblomov, the eponymous hero of Ivan Goncharov's great Russian novel, was a sweet-natured, indecisive young nobleman who didn't get out much. Didn't get out at all, in fact. Despite perfect health, he lay in bed all day — every day — contemplating his happy childhood. Nothing could raise him from his torpor until (about 200 pages into the book) his friend Stoltz briefly persuaded him to rejoin society. But Oblomov soon tired of the social whirl. Even when he fell madly in love with a pretty girl called Olga, she provided only a temporary distraction. He soon gave up on her too and went back to bed.

Oblomov is one of the more intriguing characters of world literature and much has been written about him, most of it uncomplimentary. In Russian, the word *oblomovshchina* is still used to refer to the backwardness, inertia, and futility of nineteenth-century Russian society. On the internet, 'Oblomov' is the name of a discussion list for psychologists researching 'academic and general procrastination'.

But some see Oblomov as a 'hidden and heavenly soul'. The German playwright Franz Xaver Kroetz has argued that Oblomov's 'vice' of laziness was, in reality, a virtue. 'I'll show you the life of the mind,' said the terrifying Charlie Meadows at the end of the Hollywood satire *Barton Fink* as his malevolent soul burns down the hotel. But Oblomov's soul and mind were wholly benign. He filled his 'empty' existence with dreams of paradise. Oblomov, in other words, may have been an Eastern-style mystic about a hundred years ahead of his time.

'Nothing will come of nothing,' said King Lear. In *Being and Nothingness*, Jean-Paul Sartre laid out his existentialist philosophy, exploring time, responsibility, reality and appearance and the limits of freedom. Sartre argued that existence was pointless, 'contingent' and absurd. Meanwhile, physicists and mathematicians have begun to ponder the discovery that the Void is one of the essential components of Creation: there seem to be huge amounts of Nothingness (a weird kind of matter with anti-gravity properties) which keep universes separate.

A lot of deep thinking about the Void has come from the East. Feng Shui, ikebana and T'ai Chi are all concerned with achieving harmony. The concept of yin and yang sees empty and full as balancing opposites. The emptier our minds are, the more they can be filled with the wondrous and exalted.

Lao Tze's ancient book of wisdom, *The Te-Tao Ching*, advises:

> *Take emptiness to its utmost limits:*
> *Maintain peace in the middle.*
> *The ten thousand things – side by side they appear:*
> *And through this I see their return.*
> *Things appear in large numbers:*
> *Each returns to its roots.*
> *This is called the peace.*
> *Peace: this means returning to your destination.*
> *Returning to your destination is to be eternal:*
> *Knowing eternity is wisdom:*
> *Not knowing eternity is being wild and reckless:*
> *When you are wild and reckless, your actions will lead to*
> *misfortune.*

The Void may be a principle of the East, but it has also become fashionable in the West.

Sometimes we don't want to avoid the Void. When someone gives us flowers, it's nice to have an empty vase. Finding an empty train carriage is a stroke of luck; an empty motorway is almost a miracle. Making the first pen strokes in an empty notebook or the first steps in an empty new house are sources of pure delight.

But even though the Void may be a little hip, it remains a lot scary. The truth is that our first instinct when we sense a Void opening within us is to fill it up immediately with frantic action of almost any kind. No one wants to be considered empty and, deep down, we don't really approve of Oblomov.

In *Care of the Soul: A Guide for Cultivating Depth and Sacredness in Everyday Life*, the American writer Thomas Moore warns us not to be tempted to fill this unpleasant sense of Void too quickly. A good Void, he says, can allow us to find our own strength. If we distract ourselves with meaningless activities, we will lose more than we gain.

Oblomov rejected passion and social engagement and achieved fulfilment by lying in bed in his oriental dressing-gown. Did he know something we don't?

TO DECISION AND TRUST

○ Independence

Selfconfidence
• Desire

No Trespassing

Somewhere
•

The Essence   Hermitage
Austere   ₩

PLAINS OF

SOLITUDE

• Absence
• Silence

Lonely at the Top
▲

Coming to Terms •

Transcontinental Pipeline of Transformation

MOUNTAI

MOUNTAINS OF WO

P60

SCALE   6   12   18   24   30   36

OASIS OF CALM

Contemplation

Birdsong

Breeze

Nightingale

Self-Knowing

Lack

NOWHERE

Anywhere

Satisfaction

TURNING POINT

Wasted

Grin-and-bear it

DESERT OF DESPAIR

OF WORK

Persistence

CHANGE / CHAOS

ADVERSITY

MAP 14

'I'm singin' in the rain, Just singin' in the rain ...
What a glorious feeling, I'm happy again ...
I'm laughing at clouds, so dark up above ...
The sun's in my heart, and I'm ready for love.'
Arthur Freed and Nacio Herb Brown

'In a dark time, the eye begins to see.'
Theodore Roethke

'I'm very brave generally,' he went on in a low voice:
'only today I happen to have a headache.'
Tweedledum. *Through the Looking Glass* by Lewis Carroll

When the going gets tough, the tough get going, sang Billy Ocean. Moreover, Anaïs Nin remarked: 'Life shrinks or expands in proportion to one's courage.' This doesn't necessarily apply, though, to death-obsessed depressives. In *Annie Hall*, Woody Allen's alter-ego Alvy Singer insists life is divided into two categories – the horrible and the miserable. 'The horrible would be like, um, I don't know, terminal cases, you know, and blind people, crippled. I don't know how they get through life. It's amazing to me, you know, and the miserable is everyone else. That's – that's – so – so – when you go through life – you should be thankful that you're miserable because you're very lucky to be miserable.'

The astonishing Helen Keller never thought of herself as lucky to be miserable. In the first nineteen months of her life, she was a bright and lively infant, but then she was hit by a mysterious viral infection which left her deaf, blind and desperate. 'I cannot remember how I felt when the light went out of my eyes. I suppose I felt it was always night and perhaps I wondered why the day did not come,' she recalled many years later. In her dark, silent world, Helen became uncontrollably wild, expressing her frustration through raging tantrums. When she was nearly seven, her parents hired a teacher for her called Anne Sullivan, herself the survivor of a violent and unhappy childhood. Sullivan was loving and attentive to her new charge. As she later explained: 'I wanted to be loved. I was lonesome – then Helen came into my life. I wanted her to love me and I loved her.'

From the time before her illness, Helen had retained a faint memory of light. She had also made sounds and dimly remembered the word 'wah-wah' for water. One day Sullivan took Helen to a water pump and, as she held the little girl's hands under the flow, traced the word water into her other hand several times. Suddenly, Helen understood that 'water' was the name of the liquid she felt on her hand. She stopped and touched the earth to ask its name. By nightfall, she had learned thirty words in this fashion.

Over the next fifty years, Sullivan devoted herself to Helen. She was her best friend and gateway to the world. Keller learned to read and write. Later she taught herself foreign languages, learned to lip-read by touching people's mouths as they spoke and to speak herself. Her intelligence and passion for learning became the stuff of legend. She insisted on going to college ('It was my right as well as my duty'). Sullivan spelled book after book and lecture after lecture into Helen's hand until she graduated cum laude from Radcliffe College, the first blind-deaf person ever to do so.

For the next fifty years, Keller championed women's and workers' rights and fought for the oppressed and the blind. 'Ignorance and poverty are the causes of much blindness. These are the enemies which destroy the rights of children and workmen, and undermine the health of mankind. These causes must be searched out and abolished.' She wrote thirteen books and was a frequent contributor to magazines and newspapers, writing most often on blindness, deafness, social issues, and women's rights.

Sometimes the most terrifying adversity can trigger courage and determination. In June 1940, when Hitler's blitzkrieg had just crushed France and routed the British army and many neutrals assumed Britain would have to sue for peace or face destruction, Winston Churchill combined defiance with inspiration:

> What General Weygand called the Battle of France is over. I expect that the Battle of Britain is about to begin. Upon this battle depends the survival of Christian civilization. Upon it depends our own British life, and the long continuity of our institutions and our Empire. The whole fury and might of the enemy must very soon be turned on us. Hitler knows that he will have to break us in this Island or lose the war. If we can stand up to him, all Europe may be free and the life of the world may move forward into broad, sunlit uplands. But if we fail, then the whole

CHAOS

PINNACLES OF CONFUSION

▲ 2.875   • 1.974 ▲
                        ▲ 1.679

Oblivion
Cause
NOT TO BE
Revolution
CHANGE
Transformer
Omen   CALAMITY
Damien

Armageddon
Inferno
▲
Apocalypse

SLIPPERY SL

EVOLUTION
TO BE

TO BECOME
Consequences

PROBLEMS

Unavoidable Way

Tren a Gran de Tristésse

Transcontinental Pipeline et Exist und Decay

Exhaustion

Bravery
• 3.876 ▲

PRID

Despair

MOUNTAINS   OF   DESPA

Loss

Stoic
Cry ○
Last Drop

• 4.213
▲

The Alamo •

MORTALITY

TO MEMORY
AND
DREAMS

world, including the United States, including all that we have known and cared for, will sink into the abyss of a new Dark Age made more sinister, and perhaps more protracted, by the lights of perverted science. Let us therefore brace ourselves to our duties, and so bear ourselves that, if the British Empire and its Commonwealth last for a thousand years, men will still say, "This was their finest hour."

'Courage is a special kind of knowledge: the knowledge of how to fear what ought to be feared and how not to fear what ought not to be feared,' said David Ben-Gurion. Ernest Hemingway defined courage as 'grace under pressure'.

'The only thing we have to fear is fear itself.'
Franklin D. Roosevelt

*'If at first you don't succeed, try again. Then quit. There's no use
being a damn fool about it.'*
W.C. Fields

Parachutists do it. Mountain climbers sometimes do it without meaning to. And educated
bungee-jumpers do it all the time. (But fleas never do.) As the Cole Porter song does-
n't quite go: let's fall from a very high place with a genuine risk of death or injury.

Even for the powerful, pushing physical and psychological limits can be thrilling. As a
twenty-year-old US Navy aviator on the aircraft carrier San Jacinto, the future president George Bush had bailed out of his burning torpedo bomber. Fifty-two years
later, the by-now former president Bush bailed out again — leaping from the back of a
small white plane 12,500 feet above the Arizona Desert. He plunged in freefall for a
few seconds before pulling the rip cord and floating to earth where he was greeted by
relieved security men. Three years later, Bush celebrated his seventy-fifth birthday in
similar fashion. 'It's a euphoric high,' he explained. 'You just feel wonderful. We were
rolling around in the sky, unlike the first jump, and it was heaven. It was just exhila-
rating.'

As the former president skydived, he was filmed by a legendary stunt cameraman called
Tom Sanders. Three years after the Arizona jump, Sanders found himself amid the
stunning beauty of the Yosemite National Park in California filming another para-
chutist, his wife Jan Davis, as she BASE-jumped from the top of a 3,600-foot granite
cliff called El Capitan. BASE-jumping is like normal parachute jumping, only more
dangerous. 'To put your life in danger from time to time ... breeds a saneness in deal-
ing with day-to-day trivialities,' said Nevil Shute. Or as a colleague of Tom and Jan
explained: 'Have you ever looked over the edge of a tall building or a cliff and wondered what it would be like to jump off? I wondered and now I know what it's like:
You're dead and all of a sudden you're alive again.'

Jan Davis had performed more than 3,000 sky-dives and 70 BASE-jumps and was the first
woman to leap from the world's tallest waterfall, Angel Falls in Venezuela. She had
discovered the pleasure of jumping after the death of her first husband: 'I needed
something to focus all my attention on, kind of a grief therapy,' she explained later.
'I soon became addicted and went hard core. I feel very lucky now to make my living from something I have such passion for. I truly believe it's not because things
are difficult that we don't dare; it's because we do not dare that they are difficult.'

Her Yosemite leap was part of a political protest against park authorities who had banned BASE-jumping for being too dangerous. As she threw herself from the granite cliff, she was dressed in symbolic prisoner's stripes. Because she was to be arrested and her equipment confiscated, she used a borrowed parachute. 'As far as I could tell, she looked as if she had a good, stable exit,' Sanders said later. 'There was never any tumbling. And she just continued to fall, and fall, and fall. But when she continued to fall, and once I saw the trees come into frame, I knew it was too late.' As his wife hit the ground, eye-witnesses saw the grief-stricken Sanders collapse on to his camera.

'Life is about action and passion, and you truly can't begin to live life until you overcome your fear of dying,' Jan Davis had said, and her death failed to persuade park authorities or her fellow BASE-jumpers to change their minds about the sport. Three weeks after the tragedy, Sanders and Jan's colleagues and friends held a memorial service. There was sky-jumping, the scattering of her ashes from a plane and, at sunset, a mass simultaneous parachute jump involving more than 100 people jumping from four planes.

Humans have always had a deep need to 'push the outside of the envelope', as the test pilots and astronauts of Tom Wolfe's *The Right Stuff* put it. 'Whether we call it sacrifice, or poetry, or adventure, it is always the same voice that calls,' said Antoine de Saint-Exupéry. Somewhere along the line, defying death can become a compulsion. The American mountaineer Jim Wickwire, who conquered K2 and wrote a book called *Addicted to Danger*, said: 'You get into a tight situation, you get hurt; a friend gets killed, and you think you're going to stop climbing. But, after a few weeks at home, you start planning your next climb.'

DANGER

IN THE DARK

ABROAD

WANDERING

Help

To the Limit

Fireproof

Gibberish

Wilde World

Seasoned

Comfort

Maze (in)

Ambush

Point of No Return

Renown

Surprise

Drink

THE DEEP

To Archipelago of Legends

Capt. Nemo

Blofeld

Erupt

Command

Jekyll

Frankenstein

Explode

Hyde

To Madness (Knowledge)

Stuyvesant

Columbus

Odysseus

Armstrong

Man Friday

Crusoe

Glenn

Gulliver

Livingstone, I presume

Lilliput

Barentz

Amundsen

Scott

Moby Dick

ARCHIPELAGO OF LEGENDS

Marie Celeste

Captain Ahab

Lassie

The Beagle

SCALE   10   20   30   40   50

> *'A woman drove me to drink, and I'll be a son-of-a-gun but I never even wrote to thank her.'*
>
> W.C. Fields

Few obscure historical figures loved food as much as the ill-fated Roman Emperor Vitellius. According to his enemies, Vitellius used to enjoy at least four big meals (and a drunken revel) every day. He was also in the habit of vomiting copiously to keep himself hungry and would even grab food-offerings at religious ceremonies or scoff left-overs from roadside taverns when he travelled. At one gargantuan meal for which the phrase 'huge banquet' seems a feeble understatement, his brother served up 2,000 fishes and 7,000 birds for the emperor. Another feast involved a ginormous dish known as 'Minerva's Shield' in which 'were tossed together the livers of charfish, the brains of pheasants and peacocks, with the tongues of flamingos and the entrails of lampreys, which had been brought in ships of war as far as from the Carpathian Sea and the Spanish Straits' (Suetonius). It may have been fun while it lasted, but Vitellius is remembered, if at all, as a greedy, cruel tyrant. When he was overthrown after less than a year in power, he tried to escape by disguising himself in dirty clothing but he was captured, dragged half-naked to the Forum, tortured and thrown into the Tiber. A dishonourable end for an emperor. Tacitus's verdict: 'Vitellius with his sensuality and gluttony was his own enemy.'

Another unforgettable big man with what Iggy Pop calls 'a lust for life' (for food anyway) is Mr Creosote from the French restaurant in Monty Python's *Meaning of Life*:

> Maître d': Ah, good afternoon, sir, and how are we today?
> Mr Creosote: Better.
> Maître d': Better?
> Mr Creosote: Better get a bucket ...
> (Once Mr Creosote has finished throwing up into the bucket, the waiter tempts him with 'very delicate, very subtle' delicacies: jugged hare (with a sauce made of truffles, anchovies, Grand Marnier, bacon and cream), moules marinières, pâté de foie gras, beluga caviare, eggs Benedict, leek tart, frog's legs amandine, quail's eggs on a bed of pureed mushroom ...)
> Mr Creosote: I'll have the lot.
> Maître d': A wise choice, Monsieur. And now, how would you like it served? All, uh, mixed up togezer in a bucket?
> Mr Creosote: Yeah ... with the eggs on top.
> Maître d': But of course ...

It surely signifies something or other that the word 'food' rhymes much more convincingly with 'rude', 'nude' and 'lewd' than it ever does with 'good', 'understood' or 'sainthood'. Moreover, gluttony, famously, is one of the seven deadly sins. But foodie-ness can be — and often is — next to godliness.

In literature and film, food is seldom just for eating. It is charged with emotional, spiritual or character significance. 'Leave the gun; take the cannoli,' says Clemenza in *The Godfather*. Michael Ondaatje's *Anil's Ghost* alludes to the sublime possibilities of food-giving trees: 'It was legendary that every Tamil home in Jaffna Peninsula had three trees in the garden. A mango tree, a murunga tree, and the pomegranate. Murunga leaves were cooked in crab curries to neutralise poisons, pomegranate leaves were soaked in water for the care of eyes and the fruit eaten to aid digestion.' Food is a metaphor for life in *Eat Drink Man Woman*. In $9^1/_2$ *Weeks*, the contents of a fridge become a sophisticated sex toy.

Yet food — as art and a sublime spiritual force for healing and redemption — has never seemed as beautiful as in Karen Blixen's story *Babette's Feast*. In a bleak little Scandinavian village two devoted daughters of a pastor live with Babette, a mysterious French housekeeper. The once-beautiful and gifted daughters have followed their father's puritanical teachings, eschewing all sensual pleasures and devoting themselves instead to the pastor and, later, his ageing, bickering disciples. Food in this God-fearing community is as plain and tasteless as possible: salted fish, dry bread, water, are luxury enough. When Babette wins a small fortune in a French lottery, she cooks a meal celebrating the Pastor's life. Not wishing to appear ungrateful, the congregants swear to 'cleanse our tongues of all taste and purify them of all delight or disgust of the senses, keeping and preserving them for the higher things of praise and thanksgiving'. But the meal, which evokes the Last Supper, is sublime. The blinis Demidof, *cailles en sarcophages*, turtle soup, Amontillado, Veuve Clicquot 1860, grapes, peaches, fresh figs and the other ingredients brought at great expense from Paris combine to generate a state of grace. Babette turns out to have been the greatest chef in Paris, once cook at the Café Anglais, and a supreme artist. She has blown her winnings on the single meal, but seemingly healed a lifetime of regret and self-sacrifice. Over the course of the evening, the congregants kiss and make up and the daughters are redeemed. 'Mercy and Truth have met together. Righteousness and bliss shall kiss,' says the ageing General Lowenhielm, who, as a young hussar, was rejected by one of the daughters, Martine, even though they both loved each other. He tells her:

> 'I have been with you every day of my life. You know, do you not, that it has been so?'
> 'Yes,' says Martine. 'I know that it has been so.'
> 'And,' he continued, 'I shall be with you every day that is left to me. Every evening I shall sit down, if not in the flesh, which means nothing, in spirit, which is all, to dine with you just like tonight. For tonight I have learned, dear sister, that in this world everything is possible.'

GROWTH

Las

Aperitif

Port Salut
Port Rouge
Cigarillo
Port Blanc · Quattro St

ENTRÉE
ALACARTE Marinara

Chocolate
Waferthin Mint
Mmmmm...

Mr. Creosote
Yum

Dessert
70% vol.
GRANDE
Anticl
BOUFFE
The Rocks
Petit Fours

Leftovers

Satisfaction

Lager
Summer
Sprouts
Mr. Vindaloo
Take it
Leave it
Defrost
Soup of the Day
Gel
Foie Gras
Mt. Deepfreeze
Haggis

CHOLESTEROL
Lard

Acid

Dripping
Rancid

Scratching
Gherkin
Salted
Pickle
Unsalted
Lard
Tansy
Whopper
Quarter Pounder
Doublewhopper
Fl
Filetofish
Bigmac
FAST FOO
Royalle

PLAYA DEL TAKEAWAY

SEA OF

SCALE
10 20 30 40 50

MOUNTAINS OF WORK

Two Stars

M O U T H W A T E R

To Lens Evenings

C O S T A   D E L   T H I R S T

PLEASURE

One Star

'oeuvre

Taste

Apellation Controlée

Parmesan

Home Cooking

Pinot Blanc

Pinot Noir

Al Funghi
ipasto

Waiter

Blinis
Demidof

Tart

Sweet

More Wine

Chateau
Migraine

Sour

Syrup

Pont Veuve Cliquot

Blancmange

Taste

Bain Marie

Gravadlax

Boiling Point

Mt.Chou

Roque Fort

rgonzola

F R U I T S   D E   M E R

Bouillabaisse

FISHMARKET

Aftertaste

Halitosis

utamate

Peppermint

S U S H I

Surimi

Fugu

Nori

I S L A N D S

E N T Y

Man:	*You were wonderful tonight.*
Mae West:	*I'm always wonderful at night.*
Man:	*Tonight I thought you were especially good.*
Mae West:	*When I'm good I'm very good, but when I'm bad I'm better.*
Man:	*If I could only trust you ...*
Mae West:	*You can – hundreds have.*

A friend of Jimi Hendrix received a call from the rock legend late one night. 'Come right over,' pleaded Hendrix, sounding panicky. 'I need help fast.' The friend rushed to his jeep and raced the eight miles to the star's secluded mansion in Woodstock. When he arrived, the cook told him Hendrix was upstairs in his bedroom, so the friend raced up, taking two stairs at a time, and burst into the room. Hendrix was lying spread-eagled in the middle of his huge bed, surrounded and overwhelmed by six or seven naked girls. He looked up and asked: 'You a friend?'

'Yes.'

'Do me a favour.'

'Anything.'

'Take your clothes off and join me.'

Hendrix was the greatest of all rock guitarists and a living embodiment both of Mae West's line: 'too much of a good thing can be wonderful,' and Ian Dury's lyric: 'Sex and drugs and rock and roll / Is all my brain and body need / Sex and drugs and rock and roll / Are very good indeed.' Living embodiment, that is, until he choked to death in desperate, murky, drug-assisted circumstances in September 1970. The creator of febrile music which still has the power to inspire and astonish was gone at twenty-seven.

Few milieux in human history have been as creative, recklessly experimental or as single-mindedly dedicated to hedonism as the sixties musical underground. 'If you can remember the sixties you weren't there,' as Robin Williams said. But a terrifying price was paid for the fun. Among the leading figures of the counter-culture in the sixties the casualty rate – dead, wounded or missing in action – was akin to that of an RAF squadron during the Battle of Britain. One of the epicentres of excess and excitement was the New York nightclub Max's Kansas City, hangout for the likes of Allen Ginsberg and William S. Burroughs, Roy Lichtenstein and Andy Warhol, Bob Dylan, Mick Jagger, Jim Morrison, David Bowie, Janis Joplin and the Velvet Underground. Some of the denizens of Max's were immortalised in Lou Reed's song 'Walk on the Wild Side'. But Reed later recalled: 'Few of the regulars lived long enough to be a nostalgic memory ... A young, reckless, night-time bunch we were. The dark brigade who never saw the sun.'

Such a fine line between pleasure and destruction. In the elegant black comedy, *La Grande Bouffe*, a group of wealthy middle-aged men retire to a Paris villa, where they indulge themselves in carnal pleasures until they die in a nihilistic blow-out of orgiastic over-indulgence.

And pleasure and pain have always had much more in common than their first letters. 'Pleasure only starts once the worm has got into the fruit. To become delightful, happiness must be tainted with poison,' said Georges Bataille, French documenter of sexual excess and author of books like *The Story of the Eye*, *Literature and Evil* and *L'Érotisme*. Or, as another Frenchman, that dedicated follower of passion, the Marquis de Sade, put it: 'Happiness lies only in that which excites, and the only thing that excites is crime ... I have supported my deviations with reasons; I did not stop at mere doubt; I have vanquished, I have uprooted, I have destroyed everything in my heart that might have interfered with my pleasure.'

Aristotle said: 'The aim of the wise is not to secure pleasure, but to avoid pain.' But when Hendrix sings: 'Scuse me while I kiss the sky ...' how many such 'wise men' even know what he is talking about? 'It's true I spent all my money on booze, women and gambling,' said the glorious footballer and Elvis-impersonator Frank Worthington. 'But at least I didn't waste it.'

But there are gentler and less expensive routes to a good time. The Greek philosopher Epicurus, whose name is a byword for pleasure-seeking, actually argued for moderation: 'It is not possible to enjoy if one does not practise prudence in one's pleasures.' His predecessor, the hedonist Aristippus, urged us to take pleasure in the moment.

Our senses provide intense but simple pleasures every day, if only we paid attention to them: a wonderful sunset, beautiful music, a glorious meal; a lover's caress. Playwright Dennis Potter, in his last television interview as he was dying of cancer, spoke of the extraordinary intensity of his perceptions: 'Below my window in Ross ... the blossom is out now. It's a plum tree, it looks like apple blossom but it's white, and, looking at it through the window when I'm writing, I see it's the whitest, frothiest, blossomest blossom there ever could be, and I can see it. Things are both more trivial than they ever were and more important than they ever were, and the difference between trivial and important doesn't seem to matter. But the "nowness" of everything is wondrous.'

You don't have to be dying to notice beauty, but it seems to help.

MOUNTAINS OF WORK

Disguise

Surprise

Radiant

So What?

P R A C T I C A L

Reckless

L
O
K
E
S

Cheer

Hilarious

Cheerful

Bubblins

Fast Food

B
E
A
M
I

Sparkle

Ha-Harbour

Let's do Lunch

Laughter

Day Out

Wink

Day Out at the Seaside

Twinkling Eyes

Run Riot

Brilliant

Amazing

Lu

Brea

Ovation

Meti

Apellation Controlée

Wonde

Disco

Waiter!

More Wine

H
A
U
T
E

C
U
I
S
I
N
E

To Haute Cuisine

In

Spark

Hangover

Hammock

Whisp

To Playa del Takeaway

S

S
E
A

Rock-a-Bye

O
F

Rocking

P
L
E
N
T

SCALE

50   100   150

Jealousy

Dirty Look

GOOD OLD DAYS

Cherish

Photos

Decadence

Rituals

Y E S T E R D A Y

Mouldy

HAPPY

Strolling

Old Age

Retrospective

F O R E S T S   O F   C H A N G I N G   O F   C O L O U R S

...ay Cake

...day

Binoculars

Paddle

Great Pleasure

Fabulous

Playtime

B A Y   O F

And Again

Peer

FREEDOM

Sigh

Purring

Horseplay

Happiness

C
O
N
T
E
N
T
M
E
N
T

Splash

Stroll

R
A
M
B
L
I
N
G

All Day Long

Longing

S U M M E R

Dissolute

Drowsy

Skylark

Again

Spree

Let's Go

Sundays

Lazing

Same Old Story

Walking on Air

A F T E R N O O N S

Humming

Frolic

Nostalgia

Always

SEA

Echo

Jump

Drift

OF

Fragrant

FLOWERS

Relic

...KENINGS

Honey

Experience

Cheers!

Good Friends

Superb

Drink Deeply

With Pleasure

Souvenir

...erescence

Cold Beer

Cool Breeze

Monty

Python

Mmmmm!

Ogle

B...OWSE...

Beach Ball

HOMESICK

Return

Resolute

M
O
R
T
A
L
I
T
Y

Daydreaming

Perceptive

'If the world were perfect, it wouldn't be.'
Yogi Berra

'Become a student of change. It is the only thing that will remain
constant.'
Anthony J. D'Angelo

The philosopher William James was amazed and enchanted when he first visited the
Chautauqua Institution, a fabled New York spiritual holiday resort and education centre
– a 'middle-class paradise' – which thrived in the late nineteenth century. 'The moment
you enter this holy domain, you feel the atmosphere of success,' he wrote admiringly.
'All around, you can feel modesty and diligence, intelligence and goodness, and neat-
ness and excellence, prosperity and cheerfulness.' James went to Chautauqua for a day,
but ended up staying a week, 'enchanted by the charm and convenience of it all, by this
middle-class paradise, without sin, victims, a stain or a tear.' He felt he had stumbled
into Utopia. The place was teeming with the nicest people. There were schools and
sports facilities of every kind, beautiful music was provided by a 700-voice choir in the
world's most perfect open-air auditorium. 'There are no contagious diseases, poverty,
drunkenness, crime or police and you will find culture and friendliness. Everything is
cheap and everybody is the equal of everyone else. You will find here the best of everything mankind has strived for in the name of civilisation and what it has fought and bled
for over the centuries.'

Chautauqua was, in a word, perfect. And James rapidly grew to hate it. By the time he left,
he ached for something primal, urgent and vivid. 'Give me back the large worldly jungle
with all its sins and suffering, where there are peaks and valleys, the beast and high
ideals, the splendour of all that is terrible and infinite. There you will find endlessly
more hope and help than on this level of deadly mediocrity.'

We think we yearn for the highest ideals, for 'happiness'. And we like the idea of striving
for some distant promised land. Yet whenever we reach one, it fails to satisfy. As
Robert Louis Stevenson put it: 'To travel hopefully is a better thing than to arrive, and
the true success is to labour.' We want the struggle and excitement of striving. We
need to be surprised and challenged constantly. We need blood, sweat 'n' tears, for as
soon as we've achieved our goal we are hungry for the next challenge.

We are hopelessly restless creatures, adrenalin junkies who crave ever more vivid stimuli.

As children, every day seemed filled with the wonder and joy of what we saw and experi-
enced. Little by little we discovered the world as it unfolded before our eyes. Actually
it was not the world that was fresh, but our experience of it and the intensity with
which we paid attention to it. For a child, clouds, thunder, a shadow, the ladybird that

lands on a hand, are thrilling. As we grow older, we pay less attention to the present and more to striving towards distant goals. The wonder of daily life disappears because we've seen it all before. We are no longer moved by a stranger's smile, the sun travelling across the sky, or how a clothespeg works.

An ascetic was meditating in a cave when a mouse crept inside and started nibbling his sandal. The ascetic was irritated and opened his eyes.

'Why are you disturbing my meditation?' he asked fiercely.

'I'm hungry,' squeaked the mouse.

'Go away, foolish mouse!' said the ascetic. 'I'm looking for unity with God. How dare you disturb me?'

'How can you hope to unite with God,' replied the mouse, 'when you cannot even see eye to eye with me?'

Searching for orchids, we miss the daisies. We are so used to focusing on the Future, the New, the Important and the Valuable, that everything that is ordinary and natural escapes our attention.

A man once asked the Zen master Ikkyu to write down some words of his deepest wisdom. Ikkyu wrote down a single word: 'Attention.'

'Could you add something to that?' asked the man.

Ikkyu wrote down: 'Attention. Attention.'

The man was still not satisfied and said he could find little wisdom in this.

So Ikkyu wrote: 'Attention. Attention. Attention.'

'But what does attention mean?' the man asked finally.

'Attention means attention,' said Ikkyu.

The opposite of life is not death; the opposite of life is time
Title of sculpture by Morris Graves

'I don't want to achieve immortality through my work. I want to achieve it through not dying,' said Woody Allen. Strangely, though, those who do live for ever tell us that immortality is a lot less fun than it looks. Vampires, for example, have a rotten time. No real friends; chronic allergies, a very limited diet, depression, mood swings ...

As Bram Stoker's Dracula put it: 'I seek not gaiety nor mirth, not the bright voluptuousness of much sunshine and sparkling waters which please the young and gay. I am no longer young, and my heart, through weary years of mourning over the dead, is attuned to mirth. Moreover, the walls of my castle are broken. The shadows are many, and the wind breathes cold through the broken battlements and casements. I love the shade and the shadow, and would be alone with my thoughts when I may.' His cousin Nosferatu the Vampyr, who appeared both in Murnau's masterpiece *Nosferatu. Symphony of Terror* and again, more talkatively, in Werner Herzog's film, *Nosferatu*, has spoken movingly of his plight: 'Dying is cruelty against the unsuspecting but ... it is more cruel not to be able to die ... The absence of love is the most abject pain.'

It's even worse for lesbian vampires. There may be women (and men) who'd consider eternal damnation a price worth paying for the pleasure of spending several centuries as Catherine Deneuve's lover. (Faust sold his soul for a much shorter time and for arguably less). But it's really not worth it. Afterwards you find yourself, as Deneuve's blood-drinking companions did in *The Hunger*, stuck in a very tiny wooden box for countless, fully-conscious aeons of agonising undeadness. Just say no.

Immortality is tough even when you're an angel. There are two angels, Damiel and Cassiel, in Wim Wenders' sublime *Wings of Desire*. Damiel falls in love with a beautiful trapeze artist and runs away from eternity to join the human circus, gladly exchanging his wings for true love. But what of Cassiel, who is left behind? When the lovers finally meet, Cassiel is present. Trapped in his lonely monochrome world as his friend moves to passion and technicolour, Cassiel turns his face to the wall and screams in silent despair.

'Hope I die before I get old,' sang The Who, though they didn't really mean it. Maurice Chevalier reckoned: 'Old age isn't so bad when you consider the alternatives.' Yet it is often said that ageing is entirely worse than the alternative; that the opposite of life is not death but the torment of physical and mental decay.

We live in a culture obsessed with beauty and youth. Thanks to improvements in diet and medical technology, we are living longer than at any time in recorded history. But more and more of us are living in nursing homes. As geneticists race to find ways to extend human lifespan, they are – or should be – haunted by the story of the Struldbruggs.

These were the immortals encountered on the third voyage of *Gulliver's Travels*. When Gulliver first hears of the Struldbruggs, he is delighted and assumes that their lives must be rich with wisdom. Not quite. The Struldbruggs had been denied the gift of eternal youth to go with their longevity and had aged hideously: 'They were the most mortifying Sight I ever beheld, and the Women more horrible than the Men. Besides the usual Deformities in extreme old age, they acquired an additional Ghastliness in Proportion to their Number of Years, which is not to be described ... At Ninety they lose their Teeth and Hair; they have at that Age no Distinction of Taste, but eat and drink whatever they can get, without Relish or Appetite. The Diseases they were subject to still continue without increasing or diminishing. In talking they forget the common Appellation of Things, and the Names of Persons, even of those who are their nearest Friends and Relations. For the same Reason they never can amuse themselves with reading, because their Memory will not serve to carry them from the Beginning of a Sentence to the End; and by this Defect they are deprived of the only Entertainment whereof they might otherwise be capable.'

Rainer Maria Rilke wrote:

> 'I reproach all modern religions for having presented to their faithful the consolations and extenuations of death, instead of giving their souls the means of getting along with death and coming to an understanding of death, with its complete and unmasked cruelty.' He also observed: 'There is an element of death in life, and I am astonished that one pretends to ignore it: death, whose unpitying presence we experience in each turn of fortune we survive because we must learn how to die slowly. We must learn to die: all of life is in that.'

Not only is death inevitable; it seems, also, to be necessary. Fritjof Capra, in *The Turning Point*, describes what he called 'the proper perspective on the phenomenon of death'. Cyclical self-renewal is an essential aspect of living systems. Living structures are continually replaced with living organisms. 'Birth and death, therefore, now appear as a central aspect of self-organisation, the very essence of life. Indeed, all living things around us renew themselves all the time. 'If you stand in a meadow, at the edge of a hillside and look around carefully, almost everything you can catch sight of is in the process of dying.' But for every organism that dies another one is born. Death, then, is not the opposite of life but an essential aspect of it.

Sorry, Woody.

ADVERSITY

ISSOLUTION

Resignation

MELANCHOLY

Disintegration

Irreversible

Musings

WISTFUL

Stiff

Yarns

Old-timer

Sell-by Date

Brittle

Anatevka

Conserve

Impotence

Fade

Shame

Weet and Tea

CAMOUFLAGE

Shining

Ravages of Time

Repent

Age

Regret

Maintenance Dam

SILICON

Old Wounds

Remorse

VALLEY

Reconstruction

Spectacle

Old Love

Discarded

Radiant

Beauty

Esteem

Staring
into Space

Smiles

Nostalgia

OCEAN

End

Look Back

ning

Foundations

EAWORTHY

OF

reens

Lusitania

PEACE

Farewell

Wreck

Atlantis

Love Letters

eachcomb

Bon Voyage

Message in a Bottle

'Death is the sound of distant thunder at a picnic.'
W. H. Auden

'Death is no more than passing from one room into another.'
Helen Keller

'It's tough to make predictions, especially about the future.'
Yogi Berra

Benjamin Franklin said death and taxes were the only certainties in life, but we will not experience our own death. 'Death is not an event in life,' wrote Wittgenstein. 'When we are there, death is not and when death is there we are not,' said Epicurus. So where does that leave us? Nowhere, as Epicurus would probably say a little too quickly. Wittgenstein would probably mumble something about not having the faintest idea and hold his tongue.

Death is the Great Unknown, and that does nothing to make it more popular. Unknown is unloved, after all. This would not be a problem if we could always keep it at a great distance. But we cannot. The presence of non-existence in existence, as Heidegger put it, haunts us constantly, like a shadow. We permanently risk vanishing into nothingness. And not only through death: isolation or total estrangement have a similar effect. The existential angst all this inspires need not be purely negative. It should persuade us not to squander our time, but to embrace life and to enjoy it to the full.

Near-death experiences have become a good deal more popular than death itself. People who have come back from near-misses with eternity have led us to believe our own deaths may not be so bad after all. Martha Todd, a professor of English literature at an American University, went into cardiac arrest due to an allergic reaction during a routine operation:

> I realised I was floating towards the ceiling. I could see everyone very clearly around the bed, even my own body. I thought it was strange that they were worrying about my body. I felt fine and I wanted them to know this, but there was no way in which I could make this clear to them. It was just as if a veil or a screen had been placed between me and the other people in the room. I became aware of an opening, if you can call it that. It seemed to be a deep, dark hole and I shot inside. I had no idea what was happening to me, but it was thrilling. I came through the tunnel to a place bathed in soft, bright light and filled with radiant love. This love was all around me and it even seemed to fill my deepest innerself. At a certain point, I was shown the events of my life. I was in a huge kind of

panorama. It is not really easy to explain. There were people with me in the light, people who had already died; a university friend, my grandfather, a great aunt and many others. They were radiant, happy. I did not want to go back, but a man in the light said I had to return, that I had not yet done what I had to do in life. I returned to my own body with a shock.

Other people who have spent more time in Elsewhere than Martha Todd have described how it looks. Although it is difficult for them to find the right words, these witnesses generally describe it as a delightful rural area, sometimes with beautifully coloured birds and flowers, intriguing scents, heavenly music. And there are people there: some who have already passed over, others, including friends, who are still alive, especially children.

With this alluring prospect, who wouldn't be tempted to exchange the temporary for the eternal? Yet very few of us are keen to experience it for ourselves. Is this because we do not really believe in Elsewhere and are therefore a little dubious about Near-elsewhere?

We all have our own reasons for being and for remaining here on earth. Our purpose is to pursue all that is good, true and beautiful; discover who we are; create a paradise on earth; fulfil our duty; serve God; serve our fellow humans; work out karma; earn our place in heaven; discover the divinity within ourselves. Alternatively, we must passively accept our fate and have a better time in the next life. Or – no less valuably – be part of something bigger than ourselves in politics, a career, as a lover, through having children.

In *God: A Biography*, the former Jesuit Jack Miles reached the conclusion that the Tanach, the Old Testament in its original Jewish version, showed that God had created humans in order to get to know Himself better, through His own experiences. Since all our experiences are unique, the purpose of our lives would thus be to have as many different experiences as possible in order that God would end up with a kind of Atlas of Experience.

For the moment, it's a good idea for us to get to know ourselves better, because our existence could turn into non-existence at any moment. Perhaps we can do this by examining whether our fear of Elsewhere and the Void is the Secret with which we drive away Boredom and dive into Passion, Knowledge, Mountains of Work or Pure Pleasure. Finally, we shall come Home, Recovered.

INDEX

NAME	TYPE	CHART NUMBER	PAGE
Debauchery	town	3	24
Decadence	ship	11	55
Decadence	ship	18	79
Decay	river	20	87
Decency	fortress	4	29
Decency	fortress	5	32
Decision	street	19	82
Decision	town	3	25
Deep	lake	16	70
Deep	lake	21	90
Deep	sea	2	20
Deep, the	sea	16	71
Deep Throat	territory	1	17
Defame	territory	7	40, 41
Defrost	lake	7	40
Defrost	river	17	74
Defy	river	6	37
Defy	river	7	40
Delay	town	11	55
Delay	village	3	25
Delegate	village	11	54
Delirious	village	6	37
Delusions	village	2	20
Delusions	village	8	44
Demand	town	7	40
Denial	village	21	90
Departure	village	9	48
Dependence	town	10	51
Dependent	town	3	25
Desert of Despair	territory	13	61
Design	territory	8	45
Desire	village	10	51
Desire	village	13	60
Desire	village	21	90
Desk	town	5	32
Despair	town	14	64
Dessert	town	17	74
Develop	territory	12	57
Development	village	8	45
Devise	village	3	25
Dialectics	highway	19	83
Did	noise	15	67
Didn't	noise	15	67
Difference	building	19	82
Dignity	territory	3	24
Dignity	territory	20	86
Diligence	village	2	21
Dinner is Ready	town	4	29
Dirty Linen	village	4	28
Dirty Look	village	11	55
Dirty Look	village	18	79
Disbelief	town	3	24
Disbelief	village	21	90
Discarded	village	20	87
Disclose	town	2	21
Discoloration	village	20	86
Discovered	town	3	25
Discovered	village	2	20
Discovery	town	4	28
Discovery	village	18	78
Discretion	village	3	25
Disgrace	village	3	24
Disguise	town	11	54
Disguise	town	17	78
Dishes, the	lake	4	29
Disillusion	village	3	25
Disintegration	river	20	87
Disintegration Way	road	19	82
Disorder	territory	15	67
Disorder	village	2	20
Disorganisation	territory	15	67
Dissolute	village	18	79
District in Decline	district	19	82
District under Construction	district	19	83
Distrust	town	3	25
Distrust	village	7	40
Divide	district	15	67
Do It	territory	3	25
Dogged	village	14	65
Doublewhopper	town	17	74
Doubt	road	19	82
Doubt	village	16	70
Doubting Way	road	19	82
Doubts	territory	3	25
Downpour	village	6	37
Downpour	village	7	40
Draughty	street	19	82
Dread	territory	14	64, 65
Dreary Wood	dec. forest	4	29
Dreary Wood	dec. forest	5	32
Drift	footpath	18	79
Drift	footpath	20	86
Drifter	wreck	3	24
Drifting	lake	3	24
Dripping	island	17	74
Drink Deeply	lake	18	79
Drink Deeply	lake	20	86
Driven	village	11	54
Drizzle	village	5	33
Droopy	village	5	33
Drowning	lake	3	25
Drowning	lake	16	70
Drowning	village	3	25
Drowsy	village	6	36
Drowsy	village	18	79
Drudgery	village	11	55
Drunk	village	16	71
Dumps, the	territory	5	32
Duty	town	3	25
Duty	town	11	54

E

NAME	TYPE	CHART NUMBER	PAGE
Eccentricity	town	2	21
Echo	lake	20	86
Echo	tunnel	18	79
Echo	tunnel	20	86
Ecstasy	town	8	44
Ecstasy	town	10	51
Effervescence	lake	18	79
Ehm...	village	9	48
Einstein	village	2	21
Elixir	lake	6	36
Eloquence	river	8	45
Elsewhere		21	90
Embrace	village	14	65
Emergency	town	6	36
Emotion	village	3	25
Emotion	town	10	51
Emotions	territory	4	28
Empowerment	territory	1	55
Encourage	territory	12	57
End	town	20	87
End of the Line	village	15	67
Endless	town	4	29
Endless	town	5	32
Endless Sands	beach	5	33
Ends Meet	river	11	54
Endure	footpath	6	36
Endure	village	14	65
Energy	factory	10	51
Energy	river	11	54
Enthusiasm	town	10	51
Enthusiasm	village	11	54
Entree	city	17	74
Er...	village	5	33
Er...	town	9	48
ER	village	6	36
Erm...	village	9	48
Erupt	volcano	16	71
Escape	village	11	54
Escape	village	14	65
Espionage	submarine	1	17
Essence	lake	21	90
Essence, the	lake	13	60
Esteem	town	20	87
Eternally	village	5	33
Eternity	town	21	90
Euler	wreck	2	21
Evasion	river	3	24
Everything	territory	21	90
Evidence	village	2	20
Evil	town	3	24
Evolution	district	14	64
Evolution	district	19	82
Exaggeration	river	16	70
Excess	village	15	67
Excuse	village	6	37
Execution	road	19	83
Exhausted	ruins	6	36
Exhausted	town	11	55
Exhaustion	town	14	64
Exile	frontier	7	41
Expand	territory	12	57
Expectation	town	12	56
Expectation	village	10	51
Expectation	watch-tower	11	54
Expedition	town	8	45
Experience	village	18	79
Experience	village	20	86
Experiences	village	3	24
Experiment	village	2	20
Explode	volcano	16	71
Exploit	district	12	57
Explosive	factory	12	57
Export	city	8	45
Export	city	10	51
Export	city	12	56
Express Purpose	light rail	19	82
Extension	footpath	12	56
Extreme	town	8	44
Extremely Boring Area	territory	5	33

F

NAME	TYPE	CHART NUMBER	PAGE
Fabulous	town	18	79
Fabulous	village	2	21
Facade	fortress	11	55
Faces	village	9	48
Facts	town	6	36
Fade	village	20	87
Failure	village	11	55
Fall	village	7	41
False Teeth	village	20	86
Fame	fortress	3	25
Fanfare	village	10	51
Fantasies	village	1	17
Fantasy	city	2	21
Farewell	ship	20	87
Farewell	town	4	29
Farewell	village	10	51
Fascination	town	16	70
Fast Food	city	17	74
Fast Food	village	11	54
Fast Food	village	18	78
Fatal Attraction	territory	3	24
Fear	town	7	40
Fear	town	21	90
Fear and Tremble	con. forest	14	65
Fear of Flying	town	16	70
Feeble Excuse	village	11	55
Feelings	territory	8	45
Fermat	island	2	21
Fertile Ground	territory	8	45
Fever	town	6	37
Feverish	village	6	36
Fickle	village	3	24
Fiddle	village	8	45
Fiery	volcano	8	45
Fiery	volcano	10	51
Figures	town	6	36
Filletofish	village	17	74
Filthy	town	4	28
Finally...	village	5	33
Finally	village	11	55
Fine Arts	territory	8	45
Fine Arts	territory	10	51
Fingers	village	5	32
Fireproof	volcano	16	71
Firm	town	12	57
First Impression	territory	4	29
Firstname	town	9	49
Fishmarket	city	17	75
Fit	town	6	37
Fitzroy Street	street	19	82
Flash	airport	9	48
Flashback	town	20	86
Flavouring	factory	17	74
Flight	airport	16	70
Flights of Fancy	airport	8	44
Floating	lake	8	45
Flow	canal	19	83
Flowing On	river	8	45
Flown	airport	3	24
Flown	airport	20	86
Fly in the Face of Destiny	flight path	21	90
Fly off the Handle	airport	4	28
Flying Blind	airport	15	67
Foie Gras	village	17	74
Following, the	village	5	33
Foolishness	village	11	55
Force	river	12	56, 57
Foreknowledge	village	2	21
Forest of Curiosity	territory	2	21
Forests of Changing Colours	dec. forest	20	86
Forests of Changing Colours	territory	18	79
Forge of Nefarious Plans	factory	19	82
Forgiveness	town	3	24
Formed	village	3	25
Fort Alzheimer	fortress	9	48
Fortune	road	19	83
Foul Play	town	3	24
Foundations	volcano	20	87
Fountain of Change	fountain	19	82
Fragments	territory	8	45
Fragrant	village	18	79
Frankenstein	factory	16	71
Frantic	village	5	32
Freedom	airport	11	54
Freedom	city	18	79
Frenzy	village	10	51
Frenzy	village	12	57
Frolic	village	10	51
Frolic	village	18	79
Frolic	village	20	86
Frozen Wastes		7	40, 41
Frozen Wastes	territory	6	37
Frozen Wastes	territory	7	40, 41
Fruits de Mer	sea	17	75
Frustration	town	8	45
Fugu	island	17	75
Full-Bodied	village	20	86
Full Speed Ahead	ship	6	37
Fun	town	11	54
Funeral	building	19	83
Fusion	village	2	20
Fuss	village	15	67

G

NAME	TYPE	CHART NUMBER	PAGE
Galapagos Lane	street	19	82
Gamble	village	3	25
Garbage	park	19	82
Gauss	wreck	2	21
Gelati	village	17	74
Genius	town	2	21
Get Well Soon	village	6	37
Getaway	highway	16	70
Geyser	volcano	7	40
Gherkin	village	17	74
Ghost Town	village	20	86
Gibberish	village	16	71
Giddy Heights	airport	16	70
Give	territory	10	51
Give	territory	12	56
Give Up	village	16	71
Glances	watch-tower	10	51
Glenn	village	16	71
Glimpse	lighthouse	21	90
Glowing	lighthouse	6	37
Gnashing Teeth	village	6	37
Gnashing Teeth	village	7	41
Godot	ship	12	56
Godsend	town	16	70
Going Smoothly	mountain	11	54
Going Under	tunnel	6	37
Golden Oldies	village	4	28
Good	village	3	25
Good Friends	town	18	79
Good Idea	town	8	45
Good Old Days	city	18	79
Good Old Days	city	20	86
Goodbye Hello	village	7	40
Goose Bumps	village	7	41
Gossip	village	3	24
Gossip	village	11	54
Gradual	river	10	51
Grasp	village	2	21
Gravadlax	ruins	17	75
Great Pleasure	village	18	79
Great Pleasure	village	20	86
Great Transformer, the	factory	14	64
Great Transformer, the	factory	19	82
Greater Awareness	city	3	24
Green Grass, the	territory	11	55
Greens	village	4	29
Greens	village	5	32
Grieving	territory	7	41
Grim	village	11	55
Grin and Bear it	village	11	55
Grin and Bear it	town	13	61
Gripping	town	16	70
Groan	village	6	36
Growth		12	56, 57
Growth	capital	10	51
Growth	capital	12	57
Growth	city	11	54
Guess	village	3	25
Guest	town	4	29
Guilt	village	3	24
Gulliver	village	16	71

H

NAME	TYPE	CHART NUMBER	PAGE
Ha-Harbour	village	18	78
Habit	village	3	24
Habit	village	4	29
Habit	village	5	32
Haggis	village	17	74
Halfway	village	5	33
Halfway There	village	11	55
Halitosis	village	17	75
Hallucination	watch-tower	2	21
Hammock	village	18	78
Hangout	square	19	82
Hangover	village	18	78
Happiness	city	10	51
Happiness	ship	18	79
Happiness	ship	20	86
Happy	city	18	79
Hard Road	road	19	83
Harvest	city	11	55
Haste	road	19	83
Hate	village	8	45
Hate	village	10	51
Haute Cuisine		17	74, 75
Heads-or-Tails Square	square	19	82
Health		6	36, 37
Heart	city	3	25
Heart	city	10	51
Heights of Exasperation	mountains	15	67
Heisenberg Lane	street	19	82
Help	village	16	71
Help!	town	15	67
Helpless	village	6	36
Here	city	16	70
Here	city	21	90
Hermitage	fortress	13	60
Hero	village	14	65
Hesitation	village	16	71
Hesitate	village	3	24
Hidden Flaws	village	1	17
Hide and Seek	dec. forest	3	25
Hide and Seek	dec. forest	4	28
High Demand	mountain	7	40
High Handed	mountain	7	41
High Pressure Lab	building	19	82
High Standard	fortress	2	20
Hilarious	town	18	78
Hint	village	11	54
History Repeats Itself	railway	19	83
Hmm...	village	9	48
HMS Wiles	ship	20	87
Home		4	28, 29
Home Cooking	village	17	75
Homesick	city	18	79

NAME	TYPE	CHART NUMBER	PAGE
Honey	lake	18	79
Hope	mountain	3	24
Hope	town	16	70
Hope	town	21	90
Horizon	frontier	21	90
Hors d'Oeuvre	village	17	74
Horseplay	village	18	79
Hot Chocolate	factory	4	29
Hot Water Bottle	lake	6	36
Hotbed	park	19	82
Hotch-Potch	town	15	67
Humdrum	town	4	29
Humdrum	town	5	32
Humiliation	territory	14	65
Humming	sound	4	28
Humming	village	18	79
Humming	village	20	86
Humour	town	8	45
Hunt	village	14	65
Hushhush	territory	1	17
Hyde	factory	16	71
Hype Park	park	19	82
Hypochondria	territory	6	36
Hypocrisy	town	3	24
Hypothesis	village	2	20
Hypothesis Lane	road	19	82
Hysteria	town	2	20
Hysteria	town	8	44

I

NAME	TYPE	CHART NUMBER	PAGE
(I am) the Walrus	town	7	40
i.e.	village	5	33
Icarus Airport	airport	2	20
Icarus Airport	airport	8	44
Ice-Breaker	ship	7	40
Ice Hole	lake	7	40
Iceberg Tip	island	7	40
Icing	mountain	18	78
Icy Stare	lighthouse	7	41
Idea	village	8	45
Ideals	town	3	24
Ideals	town	10	51
Ideas	district	19	82
If we...	village	5	33
Ignorance	capital	2	21
Ignore	village	7	41
Illumination	lighthouse	2	20
Illusion	village	3	24
Illusion	village	8	44
Immediately	town	3	25
Impatience	town	10	51
Impatience	town	12	56
Imperturbable	river	18	78
Implacable	village	3	24
Import	city	8	45
Import	city	10	51
Import	city	12	56
Impossibilities	village	11	55
Impossibubble	lake	14	65
Impotence	fortress	20	87
Improvisation	territory	15	67
Impulse	reservoir	19	82
Impulse	town	4	29
Impulse	village	8	45
In a Minute	village	5	33
In Conclusion	town	5	33
In Reference to	village	5	33
In the Dark	territory	16	71
In the Footsteps	footpath	16	71
Indeed	village	5	33
Independence	town	13	60
Indescribable	town	16	70
Indicated	village	6	36
Indifference	town	7	41
Inferno	volcano	14	64
Infinity	territory	21	90
Influence	district	19	83
Inimitable	road	16	70
Initiative	village	11	54
Innocence	street	19	82
Innocence	town	3	25
Inside Out	village	4	29
Inside Out	village	5	32
Insignificance	island	21	90
Insinuate	village	7	41
Inspiration Boulevard	street	19	82
Inspire	territory	12	57
Institute of Circum-stances	building	19	82
Institute of Doubt	building	19	82
Institute of Subversive Activities	building	19	82
Intense	town	10	51
Intensity	town	8	44
Intention	village	3	25
Intimate	town	18	78
Into Space	village	5	32
Into-View	lighthouse	2	20
Intuition	city	2	20
Invention	town	2	21
Invention	town	8	45
Irrational	territory	8	44
Irrelevant	town	20	86
Irrelevant	village	8	45
Irreversible	village	20	87
Isles of Forgetfulness		**9**	**48, 49**
Isles of Forgetfulness	territory	9	48, 49
Isolation	village	7	41
Itching	river	5	32

NAME	TYPE	CHART NUMBER	PAGE
Ivory Towers	building	19	82

J

NAME	TYPE	CHART NUMBER	PAGE
Jan Davis	village	14	65
Jarrett Road	road	19	82
Jealousy	town	8	44
Jealousy	town	10	51
Jealousy	town	18	79
Jealousy	village	11	55
Jekyll	factory	16	71
Jeopardy	village	14	65
Jet Lag	airport	11	54
Jet Lag	airport	12	57
Jet Lag Terminal	airport	12	57
Joke	village	9	48
Jolly	road	18	78
Jolt	volcano	16	70
Josef K. Alley	street	19	83
Jubilant	village	10	51
Judgement	town	2	21
Judgement	town	3	24
Judgement	watch-tower	3	24
Jump	village	18	79
Jump	village	20	86
Just Causeway	street	19	82
Justice	building	19	83

K

NAME	TYPE	CHART NUMBER	PAGE
Kettle	lake	4	29
Kettle	lake	5	32
Kick	town	16	70
Kiss	town	8	45
Kiss	village	10	51
Kitchen	village	4	29
Kitchen	village	5	32
Knocked	village	6	37
Knocked	village	7	40
Knowledge		**2**	**20, 21**
Knowledge	village	2	21

L

NAME	TYPE	CHART NUMBER	PAGE
Lack	village	13	61
Lager	village	17	74
Lake of Tedium	lake	5	32
Lake Plenty	lake	11	55
Lamarck Street	street	19	82
Lament	village	6	36
Lap	village	4	29
Lapse	village	3	24
Lard	river	17	74
Las Tapas	beach	17	74
Lassie	village	16	71
Last Drop	lake	14	64
Last Straw	village	14	65
Last Theorem	fortress	2	21
Later	village	3	25
Laughter	town	8	45
Laughter	town	10	51
Laughter	town	12	56
Laughter	town	18	78
Lazing	village	18	79
Lazing	village	20	86
Lazy	village	5	32
Leak	river	5	32
Leaks	village	1	17
Learn	village	3	25
Leave it	village	17	74
Left Behind	village	21	90
Leftovers	archipelago	17	74
Legends	village	21	90
Les Temps Perdus	street	19	82
Let It Be	ship	7	40
Lets Do Lunch	village	11	54
Letsdolunch	village	18	78
Let's Go	village	18	79
Let's See	village	5	33
Liberation	street	19	82
Lie	village	11	54
Lie, a	village	3	24
Light, the	lighthouse	8	45
Light, the	lighthouse	10	51
Lights, please	village	5	33
Lilliput	village	16	71
Limit	town	11	55
Linnaeus Road	street	19	82
Little Taste	river	17	74
Livingstone I Presume	village	16	71
Lonely at the Top	mountain	11	54
Lonely at the Top	mountain	13	60
Long Evenings	territory	18	78, 79
Longing	footpath	18	79
Longing	footpath	20	86
Longing	watch-tower	4	28
Look Across	watch-tower	3	25
Look At	watch-tower	3	24
Look Back	lighthouse	20	87
Look Back	watch-tower	3	24
Look Down	watch-tower	3	24
Look Out	watch-tower	3	24
Look Over	watch-tower	3	24
Look Through	watch-tower	3	24
Look Up	watch-tower	3	24
Looking Forward	lighthouse	5	33
Loser's Alley	street	19	82
Loss	city	14	64
Loss	street	19	82

NAME	TYPE	CHART NUMBER	PAGE
Lost	village	4	28
Lost	village	9	48
Lost	village	15	67
Lost Cause	wreck	4	29
Lost Cause	wreck	5	32
Lost Causeway	footpath	5	32
Lost Causeway	street	19	82
Lost Energy	village	9	48
Love	territory	10	51
Love	village	1	17
Love Letters	village	20	87
Lovebirds	airport	8	45
Low Spirits	territory	14	65
Luck	village	3	25
Lusitania	wreck	20	87
Lust	town	10	51
Lustrous	village	18	78
Luxury	town	4	29
Luxury	town	5	32

M

NAME	TYPE	CHART NUMBER	PAGE
Madness	town	2	20
Madness	town	8	44
Maelstrom	reservoir	19	83
Maelstrom	river	6	36
Mail!!	town	4	29
Main Issues	village	2	21
Maintenance Dam	dam	20	87
Maintenance Street	road	19	82
Man Friday	village	16	71
Manana	frontier	10	57
Margin	district	10	51
Margin	district	11	54
Margins	district	12	57
Marie Celeste	ship	16	71
Marinade	territory	17	74
Marinara	village	17	74
Mathematics	island	9	49
Matters Arising	village	5	33
Mature	town	20	86
Meanwhile	village	6	37
Meanwhile	village	7	40
Medicine	village	6	36
Meetings	territory	5	33
Meetings	town	11	55
Melancholy	territory	20	87
Melancholy Lane	street	19	82
Melody	city	8	45
Melting Point	town	7	40
Memo	village	11	54
Memoir	lake	20	86
Memory	village	20	86
Mess	district	15	67
Message in a Bottle	village	20	87
Metamorphosis	building	19	82
Method	town	2	20
Miasma	lake	14	65
Mine!	town	15	67
Minutes	village	5	33
Mirage	village	2	20
Mirror	lake	20	86
Mischief	town	3	25
Mischief Brewery	factory	19	82
Misfortune	road	19	83
Misgiving	village	16	70
Miss	river	5	33
Missed Stop	station	19	82
Mission Statement	village	11	54
Mistake	town	3	24
Mistakes	village	20	86
Mistress	fortress	10	51
Misunderstandings	territory	15	67
Mittens	village	4	28
Mixed Up	river	15	67
Mixing	lake	8	45
Mmmmm	village	17	74
Mmmmm!	town	18	79
Mmmmm!	town	20	86
Mnemonic Bridge	town	9	48
Moan	town	6	36
Mobile Phone	factory	11	54
Moby Dick	whale	16	71
Mockery	town	7	41
Mollycoddle	village	6	36
Monosodium Glutamate	factory	17	74
Monty	town	18	79
Monty	town	20	86
Mo(nu)ment	building	19	83
Moods	territory	8	45
Mope	river	5	33
More Wine	village	17	75
More Wine	village	18	78
Mortality		**20**	**86, 87**
Mortality	territory	20	86, 87
Mortuary	building	19	83
Mother's Day	village	9	49
Motionless	lake	18	78
Moulds	village	20	86
Mouldy	village	18	79
Mountains of Despair	territory	14	64
Mountains of Work		**11**	**54, 55**
Mountains of Work	mountains	11	55
Mountains of Work	mountains	13	60, 61
Mouths of Repugnance	bay	17	74
Mouthshut	village	11	54
Mouthwater	bay	17	75
Mouthwatering	village	4	29
Move	lake	8	45
Moving House	street	19	82

NAME	TYPE	CHART NUMBER	PAGE
Moving on	village	5	33
Mr Creosote	town	17	74
Mt Blancmange	mountain	17	75
Mt Chou	mountain	17	75
Mt Deepfreeze	mountain	17	74
Mt Gorgonzola	mountain	17	75
Mt Vindaloo	volcano	17	74
Muddle Through	sea	5	33
Murky	lake	15	67
Murmur	river	13	61
Museum of Entropy	building	19	82
Museum of Modern Art	building	19	82
Museum Park	park	19	82
Museum Square	square	19	82
Musings	town	20	87
My Vision	watch-tower	21	90
Mystery	town	2	20
Myths	town	21	90

N

NAME	TYPE	CHART NUMBER	PAGE
Names	island	9	49
Napoleon	village	14	65
Need-to-Know Base	airport	1	17
Needles	village	6	36
Neglect	town	3	25
Neglect	village	7	40
Negotiation	river	11	54
Neighbours	town	4	29
Nervous	town	16	70
Nervous Laughter	village	3	24
Nevermind	lighthouse	9	48
New Burning Bridge	town	12	56
New Perspective	lighthouse	7	40
Next Month	frontier	12	57
Next Stop	village	4	29
Next Stop	village	5	32
Next Week	frontier	12	57
Niche Marketing	village	11	55
Nightingale	town	13	61
Nimbus	street	19	82
No Trespassing	frontier	11	54, 55
No Trespassing	frontier	13	60
No Way Back	street	19	82
Nocturne	village	10	51
Non-Fiction	town	2	20
Nonsense	town	2	21
Nori	island	17	75
Normal	city	4	28
Normality	highway	5	32
Nostalgia	town	20	87
Nostalgia	village	18	79
Nostalgia	village	20	86
Not my Fault	village	11	54
Not Really	village	5	32
Not Relevant	village	5	33
Not To Be	territory	14	64
Not Welcome	village	4	29
Notes	village	8	45
Nothing	village	5	32
Notion	village	3	25
Notion	village	8	45
Nowhere	territory	13	61
Nursing	village	6	36

O

NAME	TYPE	CHART NUMBER	PAGE
Oasis of Calm	lake	13	61
Obligation	town	5	33
Oblivion	town	14	64
Observation	lighthouse	6	36
Observation	watch-tower	8	45
Obsession	village	10	51
Obverse	street	19	82
Ocean of Peace	sea	20	87
Odysseus	village	16	71
Off the Rails	light rail	2	20
Offer	harbour	12	56
Ogle	lighthouse	18	79
Ogle	lighthouse	20	86
Old Age	lake	18	79
Old Age	lake	20	86
Old Ideals	village	20	86
Old Love	village	20	87
Old Timer	village	20	87
Old Times	village	11	55
Old Wounds	village	20	87
Omen	city	14	64
Omen	district	19	83
On Edge	village	6	36
On the Doorstep	village	4	29
On the Mend	mountain	6	36
On the Rocks	inlet	3	24
One Hand	lighthouse	8	44
One Star	island	17	75
Ooze	river	5	32
Open Endings	lighthouse	5	33
Opinion	village	8	45
Opportunity	town	3	25
Opposite	village/town	8	44
Order	town	2	20
Order	town	8	45
Other, the	lighthouse	8	44
Out	cemetery	4	28
Out	island	6	37
Out of Control	town	10	51
Outlet	river	15	67
Outlook	watch-tower	16	70
Ovation	village	18	78

Name	Type	Chart Number	Page
Overflow	lake	4	29
Overflow	lake	5	32
Overflowing	lake	3	25
Overpowered	village	16	70
Overtaking	highway	11	54
Overwhelmed	village	16	70
Overwhelming	lake	8	45
Overwhelming	lake	10	51
Overwhelming	territory	21	90
Overwhelming Forest	con. forest	16	70
Overwork	district	11	54
Own Way	road	3	25
P			
Paddle	lake	18	79
Paddle	lake	20	86
Page 86	village	5	33
Painful Truth	ruins	1	17
Pale	lake	6	36
Panic	town	6	36
Paradox	town	8	44
Parmesan	town	17	75
Pass of Heroes	village	5	33
Passion		10	51
Past	city	8	45
Past Glory	wreck	11	55
Past Glory	wreck	20	86
Pastime	lake	4	29
Pastime	lake	5	32
Patience	town	5	33
Patience	village	3	25
Patience	village	4	28
Patient	town	6	37
Payslip	territory	11	55
Peaks	mountains	14	65
Peaks of Euphoria	mountains	14	65
Peek	lighthouse	4	28
Peer	lighthouse	18	79
Peer	lighthouse	20	86
Penalty	territory	3	24
Penance	village	3	24
Penguin	town	7	40
Peppermint	island	17	75
Perceive	village	8	45
Perceptive	town	18	79
Perceptivity	village	11	54
Perhaps	village	3	25
Persevere	village	5	33
Persistence	village	11	55
Persistence	village	13	61
Persuasion	village	11	54
Pessimism	village	14	65
Petit Fours	village	17	74
Phobia	town	6	36
Photos	village	18	79
Photos	village	20	86
Pickle	village	17	74
Pie in the Sky	mountains	11	55
Pigsty	town	4	28
Pillar	town	11	55
Pincode	village	9	48
Pinnacles of Confusion	mountains	14	64
Pinot Blanc	town	17	75
Pinot Noir	village	17	75
Pipeline of Existence and Decay	pipeline	14	64
Pipeline of Existence and Decay	pipeline	19	82
Pipeline of Existence and Decay	pipeline	20	87
Pipeline of Non-Existence	pipeline	19	82
Pipeline of Trans-formation	pipeline	8	45
Pipeline of Trans-formation	pipeline	11	55
Pipeline of Trans-formation	pipeline	12	57
Pipeline of Trans-formation	pipeline	13	60, 61
Pipeline of Trans-formation	pipeline	19	82
Pisa	fortress	20	87
Pity	village	10	51
Pity	village	14	65
Plains of Solitude	territory	11	54, 55
Plains of Solitude	territory	13	60
Plans	city	3	25
Plaster	village	6	36
Play	city	10	51
Playa del Takeaway	bay	17	74
Playtime	village	3	25
Playtime	village	4	28
Playtime	village	18	79
Pleasure		18	78, 79
Plot	village	1	17
Plot	village	7	40
Plunge	village	16	70
Poetry	river	10	51
Point 1	village	5	33
Point 2	village	5	33
Point of No Return	village	16	71
Point of Order	village	5	33
Point Out	village	5	33
Pointless	village	4	29
Pointless	village	5	32
Poison Pens	river	7	40
Pont Veuve Cliquot	bridge	17	75
Poor Prospects	watch-towez	4	29
Poor Prospects	watch-tower	5	32
Port Blanc	village	17	74
Port Rouge	village	17	74
Port Salut	village	17	74
Possibubble	lake	14	65
Post	town	11	55
Potbelly	territory	17	74
Potential	territory	12	56
Potter Around	village	5	33
Pottering	territory	4	28
Power	fortress	3	24
Power	village	11	54
Practical Joke	dec. forest	11	54
Practical Jokes	territory	18	78
Prescription	village	6	36
Present	city	8	45
Presentation	village	11	54
Pressure	village	11	54
Presupposing	village	2	20
Pride	mountains	14	64, 65
Pride	village	3	25
Primeval Soup	lake	19	82
Private Area	territory	20	87
Problems	territory	14	64
Proclaim	village	2	20
Proclaim	village	8	44
Procrastinate	street	19	82
Profit	district	11	54
Profit Centre	district	12	57
Proliferate	territory	12	57
Proliferation	dec. forest	15	67
Promise	town	8	45
Promise	town	10	51
Propaganda	territory	3	24
Propose	town	10	51
Pros	town	11	54
Prospectus	village	11	55
Prosperity	village	11	55
Protest	village	11	54
Provocation	building	19	83
Punchline	village	9	48
Purification	factory	3	25
Purity	lake	3	25
Purring	village	18	79
Push	village	3	25
Pushback Frontiers	border	2	20
Puzzle	mountains	2	20
Python	village	18	79
Python	village	20	86
Q			
Quake	volcano	14	65
Quality	village	20	86
Quantum Uncertainty St	street	19	82
Quarantine	territory	6	36
Quarter Pounder	village	17	74
Quattro Stagione	village	17	74
Quench	lake	6	36
Quest	territory	14	65
R			
Radiant	lake	18	78
Radiant	lighthouse	20	87
Radical	town	2	20
Rain	village	7	40
Rambling	territory	18	79
Rambling	territory	20	86
Rampant	village	20	86
Rancid	town	17	74
Random	town	15	67
Range of Education	territory	2	21
Rapids	river	16	70
Rate	street	19	83
Ravaged	village	6	37
Ravaged	village	7	40
Ravages of Time	mountain	20	87
Raving	territory	2	20
Raving	village	8	44
Ray of Hope	lighthouse	6	36
Reaction	territory	3	25
Recalcitrant	village	7	40
Receipt	village	11	55
Receive	territory	10	51
Receive	territory	12	56
Reception	town	5	33
Reckless	town	3	25
Reckless	town	18	78
Reckless Heights	mountains	8	44
Reckless Heights	mountains	10	51
Recognition	village	4	28
Recognition	village	8	45
Recollect	territory	20	87
Reconstruction	town	20	87
Recovery	hospital	19	83
Red-handed	village	4	28
Refer	village	5	33
Reflection	lake	3	25
Reflection	lake	8	45
Reflection	square	19	82
Reformation	building	19	82
Reformation Square	square	19	83
Refuge	airport	6	36
Refuge	fortress	1	17
Regret	lake	20	87
Regular	territory	4	29
Regular	territory	5	32
Rejection	town	7	41
Relevant	village	20	86
Relic	village	18	79
Relic	village	20	86
Relief	village	6	36
Relief	village	14	65
Reluctance	road	11	55
Reluctant	mountain	5	32
Remedy	territory	6	36
Reminiscence	territory	20	86
Remorse	village	7	40
Remorse	village	20	87
Rendez-vous	village	8	45
Rendez-vous	village	10	51
Renown	village	16	71
Repent	village	20	87
Repetition	town	8	45
Reputation	village	3	25
Requiem	village	20	86
Resentment	village	7	41
Reserves	ruins	6	37
Reserves	ruins	7	40
Reservoir	lake	3	25
Reservoir	lake	4	28
Resign	village	11	55
Resignation	village	20	87
Resistance	fortress	6	37
Resolute	town	18	79
Respect	town	21	90
Responsibility	village	11	54
Retroactive Effect	factory	19	82
Retrospective	village	18	79
Retrospective	village	20	86
Return	town	18	79
Returning to	village	5	33
Reunion	town	4	28
Reveal	town	15	67
Revelation	town	2	20
Reverie	airport	2	21
Reverse	street	19	82
Revile	village	7	41
Revision	district	19	82
Revision	village	2	21
Revision	village	3	24
Revive	town	6	37
Revolution	district	14	64
Revolution	district	19	82
Reward Building	building	19	83
Rife	village	20	86
Ripple	street	19	82
Risk	town	3	25
Risk	town	11	54
Risk Building	building	19	83
Ritual	village	21	90
Rituals	village	20	86
Rivals	wrecks	12	56
Rock-a-Bye	island	18	78
Rocking	island	18	78
Rocks, the	mountain	17	74
Roque Fort	fortress	17	74
Round the Back	footpath	4	28
Rouse	village	16	71
Routine	city	5	33
Routine	river	5	33
Royalle	village	17	74
Rubbish	river	15	67
Rubble	territory	15	67
Ruddy	village	6	37
Ruffle	reservoir	19	83
Ruins	ruins	15	67
Rule	district	15	67
Rummage	town	4	28
Run its Course	river	5	33
Run Riot	fortress	17	74
Run Riot	ship	18	78
Run Wild	river	2	21
Running Water	river	4	28
S			
Safe	town	4	29
Safe Haven	bay	4	29
Safe Haven	bay	10	51
Safe Haven	bay	12	56
Safety	territory	4	29
Safety	territory	5	32
Salted	village	17	74
Salvage	lake	15	67
Same Old Story	village	18	79
Same Old Story	village	20	86
Sanctuary	fortress	7	40
Satisfaction	town	11	55
Satisfaction	town	13	61
Satisfaction	village	17	74
Scent	town	8	45
Scherzo	village	10	51
Science	territory	2	20, 21
Scorched Earth	territory	3	24
Scratching	village	17	74
Sea of Fervour	sea	2	20
Sea of Fervour	sea	8	44
Sea of Flowers	territory	18	79
Sea of Plenty	sea	17	74, 75
Sea of Plenty	sea	18	78, 79
Sea of Possibilities	sea	1	17
Sea of Possibilities	sea	4	28
Searching	dec. forest	6	36
Seasoned	village	16	71
Seaworthy	sea	20	87
Seclusion	fortress	2	21
Secrets		15	67
Security	watch-tower	4	29
See: told you so	lighthouse	2	21
See-Saw	village	3	25
See-Saw	village	4	28
Seething	reservoir	19	82
Self-confidence	town	2	20
Self-confidence	town	11	54
Self-confidence	town	13	60
Self-Knowing	town	13	61
Self-organisation	village	2	20
Sell-by Date	town	20	87
Sensible	territory	5	33
Serenade	sound	10	51
Serious	village	21	90
Seventh Seal	building	19	83
Shaking	town	7	41
Shame	town	3	24
Shame	town	20	87
Sharp	mountain	7	41
Sharp-Witted	territory	2	20
Shatter	town	15	67
Shells	beach	20	87
Shelter	bay	6	37
Shimura	wreck	7	41
Shining	lighthouse	20	87
Shining Light	lighthouse	21	90
Shiver	territory	6	37
Shiver	territory	7	40
Shock	storm	16	70
Shopping Channel	village	5	32
Shouted Down	noise	15	67
Show Off	village	16	70
Showing the Door	footpath	4	29
Shrink	river	20	86
Sickly	village	6	36
Side Effect	river	6	36
Side Issues	town	2	20
Side Issues	town	8	44
Sidetrack	light rail	2	20
Sigh	village	18	79
Sigh	village	20	86
Sighs	village	10	51
Sign	lighthouse	6	36
Sign	village	11	54
Silence	sound	13	60
Silence	village	8	45
Silence	village	10	51
Silicon Valley	territory	20	87
Similarities	village	8	44
Sink in	lake	8	45
Sinking	swamps	4	29
Sip	lake	5	33
Sip	lake	11	55
Sip	village	20	86
Sipping Wine	village	4	29
Siren	lighthouse	6	36
Skimping	town	15	67
Skulking	dec. forest	3	24
Skylark	village	18	79
Slacker	village	3	25
Slander	village	7	41
Sleeping in	town	4	28
Sleepy	bay	6	37
Slip	lake	7	40
Slippers	village	4	28
Slippery Slope	territory	14	64, 65
Slither	village	7	40
Slough of Despond	territory	14	65
Slow Decline	river	20	86
Slow Stream	river	20	86
Sluggish	town	4	29
Sluggish	town	5	32
Slurping	village	4	29
Sly	village	3	25
Smelling Salts	town	6	37
Smile	town	8	45
Smile	town	10	51
Smile	village	20	87
Smithereens	islands	20	86, 87
Smithereens	village	15	67
Smother	village	4	29
Smoulder	volcano	3	24
Smuggling Route	road	14	65
Snail's Pace	road	20	86
Snappy	town	4	28
Sniffle	village	6	37
Sniffle	village	7	40
Snug	town	4	29
So...	village	5	33
So What?	village	18	78
Soaked	village	16	70
Soap Opera	factory	5	33
Soggy	village	5	32
Solace	village	14	65
Solid as a Rock	beach	6	36
Solid as a Rock	village	5	33
Solution	lake	8	45
Somewhere	town	11	55
Somewhere	town	13	60
Songbird Field	park	19	82
Soon	frontier	12	57
Soon	town	3	25
Soon	town	4	29
Sophie Germain	wreck	2	21
Sorbet	lake	17	74
Sorrow	district	19	83
Sort Out	territory	15	67
Sound	territory	8	45
Soup of the Day	lake	17	74
Sour	town	17	75
Sour Grapes	village	3	24
Source	town	20	86
Source of Exasperation	lake	5	33
Sources of Inspiration	territory	8	45

Name	Type	Chart Number	Page
South Suburbia	village	5	33
Souvenir	village	18	79
Souvenir	village	20	86
Sparkle	lake	18	78
Sparkling	lake	6	37
Sparks	lake	18	78
Sparks	volcano	8	45
Sparksfly	volcano	8	44
Sparksfly	volcano	10	51
Spectacle	fortress	20	87
Speculate	village	2	20
Speechless	village	8	45
Spine Chilling	village	7	41
Spite	town	3	24
Splash	lake	3	25
Splash	lake	18	79
Splendour	lake	20	86
Sprawl	village	4	29
Spree	village	18	79
Spree	village	20	86
Sprouts	village	17	74
Spur on	light rail	3	24, 25
Spur on	light rail	12	57
Spurt	town	12	56
Squeal	village	7	40
Stab-in-the-Back	island	7	41
Stadium	stadium	19	82
Stairway to Heaven	territory	21	90
Stamping Ground	village	18	79
Stamping Ground	village	20	86
Standing By	lighthouse	5	32
Staring	village	5	32
Staring into Space	village	20	87
Startle	village	8	45
State of Dissolution	territory	20	86, 87
Statement	village	8	45
Steadfast	village	20	86
Stealth	territory	1	17
Steam	lake	7	40
Steps	district	19	82
Stiff	town	20	87
Stifle	village	5	33
Stimulate	territory	12	57
Stimulating	town	10	51
Stimulating	village	12	56
Stock	district	10	51
Stock	district	11	54
Stock	district	12	57
Stock Exchange	building	19	82
Stoic	town	14	64
Store	district	12	56
Stormy	lake	8	45
Stormy	lake	10	51
Stormy Coast	bay	6	37
Stormy Coast	bay	7	40
Strait of Umm	strait	9	48
Straits of...	strait	9	49
Strategy	village	1	17
Stream of Adrenaline	river	16	71
Stream of Ideas		**8**	**44, 45**
Stream of Ideas	river	2	20, 21
Stream of Ideas	river	8	45
Stream of Inspiration	river	8	45
Stream of Poison	river	7	41
Stream of Sub-consciousness	river	3	24
Stream of Words	river	8	45
Street of Chaos	street	19	82
Stress	city	11	54
Stroll	town	18	79
Strolling	footpath	18	79
Strolling	footpath	20	86
Struggle	village	6	37
Struggle	village	7	40
Stubborn	village	7	40
Stuyvesant	village	16	71
Styx	river	21	90
Subconscious	river	8	45
Subconsciousness	river	10	51
Submerged	submarine	3	24
Subterfuge	airport	11	54
Suburbia	town	5	33
Suburbia Falls	village	5	33
Suburbia Harbour	lighthouse	5	32
Suburbia North	village	5	33
Suburbia-on-Routine	village	5	33
Suburbia-on-Sea	town	5	32
Suburbia Parkway	village	5	33
Suburbia River	village	5	32
Suburbia-West	village	5	32
Success	city	11	54
Suffer	village	14	65
Suicide Towers	building	19	82
Sultry	village	18	78
Sum up	village	5	33
Summer Afternoons	territory	18	79
Sunday Afternoon	town	4	29
Sunday Afternoon	town	5	32
Sundays	town	18	79
Sundays	town	20	86
Superb	village	18	79
Superb	village	28	86
Superstition	village	3	24
Supply	river	6	36
Supply	district	12	57
Supposedly Everything under Control St	highway	19	83
Suppress	village	6	37
Surge	reservoir	19	83
Surgery	town	6	36
Surimi	island	17	75
Surname	village	9	49
Surprise	town	18	78
Surprise	village	11	54
Surprise	village	16	71
Surrender	town	8	44
Surrender	town	10	51
Surrender	village	7	40
Survey	town	2	21
Survey	watch-tower	3	24
Survival of the Fittest	building	19	82
Sushi Islands	islands	17	75
Suspicion	town	16	70
Swallow	lake	5	33
Swamps of Boredom	swamps	5	32, 33
Sweat	lake	14	65
Sweating	river	6	36
Sweet	town	17	75
Sweet Nothings	territory	10	51
Swept Away	village	16	70
Symbiosis	village	20	86
Symbols	village	2	20
Symbols	town	8	44
Symphony	town	8	45
Symphony	town	10	51
Symptom	village	6	36
Synthesis	district	19	83
Syrup	river	17	75

T

Name	Type	Chart Number	Page
Take it	town	17	74
Talent	mountain	3	25
Tall Stories	town	14	65
Tall Stories	town	16	70
Tangle	town	15	67
Tangy	river	17	74
Taniyama	wreck	2	21
Tapping	lake	5	32
Target	village	3	25
Tart	village	17	75
Tasks	village	11	54
Taste	river	17	74, 75
Taste	town	8	44
Taunt	river	7	41
Tea Time	lighthouse	4	29
Tea Time	lighthouse	5	32
Tears	river	8	45
Tears	river	10	51
Tease	village	5	33
Tender	village	8	45
Tender	village	10	51
Tension	city	11	54
Terrified	river	16	70
Test	village	2	20
Test	village	9	49
Testlab 1	building	19	82
Testlab 2	building	19	82
Tests	town	6	36
Tête-à-Tête	village	10	51
Thaw	territory	7	40
There	town	21	90
Therefore	village	5	33
Thesis	district	19	82
Thin Ice	lake	7	40
Thin Veneer	village	3	24
Things	island	9	48, 49
Thingy	island	9	48
Threshold	district	19	82
Ticket Office	village	5	32
Tickle	village	4	28
Ticks	village	16	71
Tidy	village	4	29
Tight Corner	bridge	14	65
Time	village	9	48
Tiny	village	3	25
Tip of the Tongue	village	9	48
Titanic	wreck	7	40
TLC	town	6	36
to Adventure	ship	5	33
to Archipelago of Legends	ship	16	71
To Be	territory	14	64
To Become	territory	14	64
to Dark Fantasy	ship	1	17
to Distaste	ship	5	32
to Excuse	ship	3	25
to Fear and Tremble	road	16	70
to Haute Cuisine	ship	18	78
to Here	ship	21	90
to Long Evenings	ship	17	75
to Madness (Knowledge)	ship	16	71
to Memory and Reminiscence	ship	9	48
to Playa del Takeaway	ship	18	78
to Pleasure	ship	21	90
to Recovery	ship	16	70
to Reunion	route	7	40
to Reunion	ship	4	29
to Secrets	ship	5	33
to Secrets	submarine	2	21
To-the-bottom	inlet	2	20
To the Limit	village	16	71
to There	flightpath	21	90
Toast	town	4	29
Toast	town	5	32
Today	frontier	12	57
Tomorrow	frontier	12	57
Top of the Pile	mountain	3	25
Top-secret	mountain	2	21
Top Secret	mountain	1	17
Tough	territory	16	70, 71
Towards Infinity	lighthouse	16	70
Towards Infinity	lighthouse	21	90
Tower of Babel	ruins	15	67
Tower of Strength	lighthouse	5	33
Tower of Strength	lighthouse	5	33
Tracked Down	river	15	67
Trackdown	river	2	21
Trade	highroad	12	56, 57
Trade	road	12	56, 57
Trade	street	19	83
Tradition	district	19	82
Traditional	fortress	4	29
Traditional	fortress	5	32
Traffic Jam	highway	11	55
Train à Grande Tristesse	light rail	14	64
Train à Grande Tristesse	light rail	19	82
Traitor	island	7	40
Transform	river	20	86
Transformer House	building	19	82
Transparent	lake	8	45
Treasure	ruins	15	67
Tree House	wood	3	25
Tree House	wood	4	28
Trek	mountains	14	65
Tremble	town	6	37
Tremble	town	7	40
Trembling	village	7	41
Trial	district	19	83
Trick	town	3	24
Tricks	town	16	70
Triumph	territory	14	65
Trouble	village	6	36
Troubled Waters	lake	15	67
Troublemaking Plant	factory	19	82
Truant	village	3	25
Trudge	river	5	32
True Nature	territory	4	28
Trust	lighthouse	1	17
Trust	town	3	25
Truth, the	territory	21	90
Turbulence	river	15	67
Turbulent	lake	8	44
Turbulent	lake	10	51
Turmoil	lake	3	24
Turmoil	town	6	36
Turning Point	city	11	55
Turning Point	city	13	61
Twice Daily	ferry	6	36
Twinkling Eyes	lighthouse	16	70
Twist	river	5	32
Twisted	village	7	40
Two Stars	island	17	75

U

Name	Type	Chart Number	Page
U-Turn	road	19	82
Ugly	town	10	51
Ugly	village	8	45
Ulcer	lake	6	36
Ultimate	town	21	90
Um...	village	5	33
Unavoidable Way	road	14	64
Unbelievable	village	2	20
Uncertainty	territory	3	25
Uncertainty Street	street	19	82
Unconditional	town	10	51
Unconscious	territory	6	37
Undercurrent	bay	2	20
Undercurrent	bay	8	44
Unknown	village	2	20
Unknown Soldier	town	14	65
Unknown Territory	territory	16	70, 71
Unlearn	village	3	25
Unsalted	town	17	74
Unshakeable	village	3	24
Untouched	village	3	24
Up the Creek	village	14	65
Up to you	village	3	25
Uplift	airport	10	51
Uplift	airport	12	57
Utmost	village	8	44

V

Name	Type	Chart Number	Page
Venture	gates	12	57
Verification	village	2	20
Vigilance	lighthouse	4	29
Violation	village	3	24
Virtue	town	3	25
Virtue	village	5	33
Virtuoso	town	10	51
Vision	town	2	21
Vision	town	3	24
Visions	watch-tower	16	70
Visions	watch-tower	21	90
Visiting Times	village	6	36
Visitors	town	4	29
Vitamin	town	6	36
Vocation	village	3	24
Void, the		**13**	**60, 61**
Void, the	territory	11	55
Voicemail	village	11	54
Volcanoes of Passion	territory	8	44
Vomit	volcano	6	36
Voyeur	lighthouse	10	51
Vulnerable	city	8	44
Vulnerable	city	10	51

W

Name	Type	Chart Number	Page
W. Allen	village	2	21
Waferthin Mint	town	17	74
Wait	village	5	33
Wait	village	10	51
Waiter!	village	17	75
Waiter!	village	18	78
Waiting	town	12	56
Walking on Air	airport	18	79
Wall, the	village	4	28
Wallow	lake	6	36
Wandering	footpath	5	32, 33
Wandering	territory	16	71
Warm Front	frontier	7	40
Warning Signs	village	6	37
Warning Signs	village	7	40
Wash	river	11	55
Washed Out	village	11	55
Waste	town	15	67
Wasted	village	13	61
Wavering	airport	10	51
Waving	lake	3	25
Wayside	village	4	29
Wayside	village	5	32
Weak	village	4	29
Weak	village	5	32
Wealth	bay	11	55
Wear and Tear	footpath	20	87
Weather	district	19	82
Weatherbeaten	street	19	82
Weeding	town	15	67
Welcome	town	4	29
Well...	town	5	33
Whatever	village	9	48
Whatsisname	village	9	49
Where was I...	village	5	33
Where were we...	village	5	33
Whereby...	village	5	33
Which Islands?	sea	9	48
Whine	village	5	33
Whirl	reservoir	19	83
Whirlpool	sea	6	36
Whirlwind	village	6	37
Whirlwind	village	7	40
Whisper	village	18	78
Whopper	village	17	74
Wide World	watch-tower	16	71
Wild	village	16	70
Wild Panic	village	15	67
Wilder	village	16	70
Wildest	village	16	70
Will	road	11	55
Windswept	town	6	37
Windswept	town	7	40
Wine	lake	20	86
Wings	village	21	90
Wink	village	18	78
Wisdom	town	2	21
Wish	town	2	21
Wish	town	3	24
Wistful	territory	20	87
Witches' Cauldron	lake	15	67
With Pleasure	village	18	79
With Pleasure	village	20	86
Withstand	village	6	36
Witness Protection Program	town	1	17
Wonder	town	18	78
Wonder	town	21	90
Wonderful Journey, a	light rail	18	78
Worse	village	16	70
Worst, the	village	16	70
Wreck	wreck	20	87
Wrinkle	river	20	86
Writer's Block	building	19	82
Wrong	village	5	32
Wrong Queue	footpath	5	32
Wrongside of Bed	village	4	28

X

Name	Type	Chart Number	Page
X-Files	town	1	17

Y

Name	Type	Chart Number	Page
Yarns	village	20	87
Yawn	village	5	33
Yearning	lighthouse	5	32
Yearning	village	2	21
Yesterday	territory	18	79
Yesterday	territory	20	86
Your Name	village	9	49
Yours!	town	15	67
Youth	territory	3	25
Youth	territory	4	28
Yum	village	17	74
70% Vol.	lake	17	74
1917 Square	square	19	82